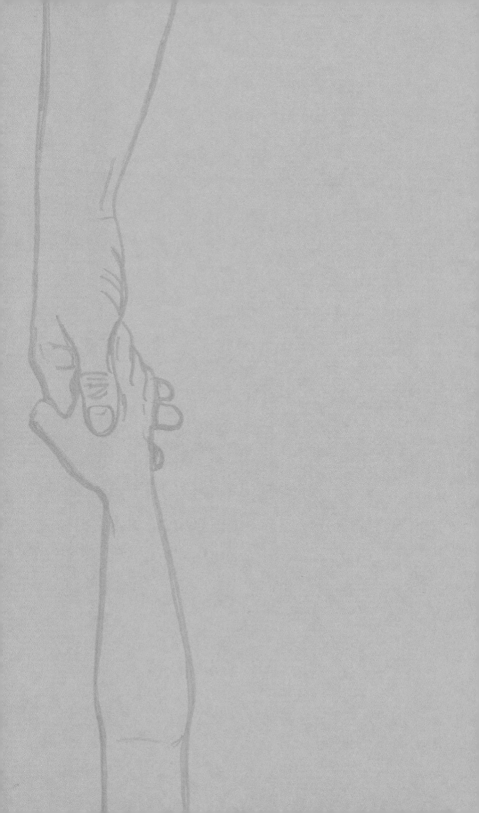

BEN MAXSON

GET NORMAL

How partnering with God transforms your life

Book concept by Jean-Luc Lézeau
Adapted and edited by Nathan Brown
Copyedited by Kathy Chee
Design and photography by Nathan Chee, Kathy Chee
Cover design by Jean-Luc Lézeau, Nathan Chee, Kathy Chee
Page 5 © Dawn Mayfarth–iStockphoto.com

Foreword

Stewardship is one of the most misunderstood and unappreciated terms in the Christian vocabulary, though politicians are not shy from using it when they want to communicate their commitment and credentials as able leaders of governments to manage the resources of their countries. But say it in certain situations in the context of the church and people will think that you're talking money—or, more specifically, tithe and offerings. For these church members, stewardship is a dated concept; an antique from another era and generation of the Christian church. This failure to see the depth and larger picture of stewardship in the church today is very unfortunate, but at the same time, it provides a wonderful opportunity to present a wholistic and refreshing paradigm on the subject grounded and informed by the Word of God.

In this book, Dr Benjamin Maxson—pastor, author and former Director of Stewardship for the General Conference of the Seventh-day Adventist Church—explores the richness of stewardship from a biblical perspective. He seeks to broaden our understanding of stewardship, and challenges us into a life of Christian living and relevance. More importantly, he invites the reader into a transformed life of discipleship and connection with Jesus Christ.

Correctly understood, stewardship is about "responsibility and service." It's about partnership with Christ and the joy of living out the real you in the presence and power of God in the here and now.

This work was first presented as a series of lectures in a seminar-style format filmed for later use in stewardship training programs for church leaders, but the content was invaluable that we felt as department of the General Conference that we needed to preserve these biblical principles and concepts and share them with the larger faith community of the church in a way that it is relevant specifically to young adults in the church today.

To assist us in this book project, we called upon the expertise and experience of individuals who in their life and ministry interact freely with our target audience. It was at this point in the process that we invited Nathan Brown (editor) and designers, Nathan and Kathryn Chee, from Signs Publishing Company in Australia to partner with us on this assignment. We're grateful for their professional support. This work would not have been completed without the perseverance and focused attention given to it by Jean-Luc Lézeau, Associate Director of the department.

As you read and journey with us on this spiritual experience of knowing God personally and allowing Jesus to be Lord of every facet of your life, our prayer is that you will find joy and peace in your heart that will transform you from inside out.

Erika F Puni
Director of Stewardship
General Conference of Seventh-day Adventists

Contents

REALITIES

Chapter 1

Not long ago, I was talking with a new friend at a seminar I was leading.

He said to me, "Ben, the kind of life that you are describing is impossible for me."

"What do you mean?" I asked.

"I don't have time to have that kind of relationship with God," he explained. "I pastor 10 churches and beyond that, we have another 15 groups. I wake up in the morning, I am busy, I have to get going and I never really have time for the kind of life you are talking about."

It seems to me like there is something wrong with a pace of life that says, "I don't have time for God"—even for those busy doing "God's work."

But perhaps the only difference is he was willing to admit it. For most of us in everyday life, the rhythm of our lives is such that often we don't have the time with God we would like to have either.

Many of us feel we are missing something from our spiritual lives, so what does "normal Christianity" look like? What does it mean to walk with God in a radically different way? Is there a biblical model that can inform us and help us?

OFTEN WE DON'T HAVE THE TIME WITH GOD WE WOULD LIKE TO HAVE.

God's realities

Yet this is not a rare experience. I have seen it many times. Several years ago, I had a pastor driving with me to a committee meeting. As I listened to him and

3

we began to talk, I heard him say something I could not believe. He said, "God expects more of me as a pastor in order to be saved than he does the average church member."

We tend to have this idea that the more we know, the more God expects from us. That may be true for service but are there different ways of being saved?

As we continued to talk, I asked him, "Are you telling me that God has one way to save a church member and a different way to save you?"

"Well, isn't that true?" he responded.

"In other words, you are saying the average church member is saved by faith but I have to earn a little bit of salvation by working harder, right?"

NO WONDER HE TURNED PALE AND BEGAN TO WEEP.

No wonder he turned pale and began to weep.

"Ben, how can it be?" he continued. "I have taught righteousness by faith and I have taught people to accept salvation as a gift, and yet I didn't internalize it into my own life."

The next morning he phoned me at 6:30.

"Ben, I hope I didn't wake you," he began. "I spent the past hour and a half lying here in bed with my wife, telling her what I went through yesterday and I am so excited."

God wants every one of us to have an exciting, vibrant, dynamic walk with Him. And yet that's not what the average Christian experiences today.

Beyond the gold-gilt frames

Some time ago, I had the opportunity to present the material of this book for a filmed production. In preparing to do that, I was privileged to work with a set designer by the name of Lousan Andanalve, who is an Adventist church member who lives near the General Conference headquarters in Silver Spring, Maryland in the United States.

Lousan immigrated to the United States from Bulgaria. His primary profession and gift is design work. He has worked with the Kennedy Center in Washington DC, designing sets and stages, then building them. He works skillfully with plastic, metal, wood and cloth.

When we talked to him about the subject of the seminar—letting God be Lord of every part of our lives—he told us that when he first came to America he saw all the large, nice houses and decided these people must be ready to meet Jesus. But he came to realize the emptiness of so many of these houses.

As he designed our set, he used gold panels to reflect on the kind of things that fancy houses would have. He also used picture frames with gold gilding—the kind of picture frames you would find in expensive houses—and extravagant pillars.

But the panels were only panels; there was no wall. And the pillars were only pillars; they did not hold anything up and there was nothing on them. And the picture frames were empty and even a little off square suggesting that life focused only on material possessions has something missing.

As you looked at the set, when you looked beyond the golden panels, the pillars, the picture frames, you saw white curtains lit with a blue light, moving upward, lifting our eyes beyond the things

THE PICTURE FRAMES WERE EMPTY AND EVEN A LITTLE OFF SQUARE SUGGESTING THAT LIFE FOCUSED ONLY ON MATERIAL POSSESSIONS HAS SOMETHING MISSING.

of this world to a spiritual dimension. Lousan was trying to help us see that we must look beyond ourselves, reach beyond the material world and find God to bring balance to everyday life.

The "s" word

So how can God become more real in our lives?

First of all we want to explore what it does mean to have a normal Christian life. We want to discover an answer in Scripture for the hunger that is in so many hearts and to see how God can reach in and make a difference in everyday life today.

We are going to do that by exploring some key points of stewardship. Of course, when I say the word stewardship the first thing that comes to mind is money. It's as if I have just attacked the most sensitive nerve in your body. There seems to be a direct connection between the wallet and the pain center of the brain. And when the preacher announces that next week we are going to have a sermon on stewardship, that's the week we decide we are going to visit another church.

WE WANT TO EXPLORE WHAT IT DOES MEAN TO HAVE A NORMAL CHRISTIAN LIFE.

But the word itself, *steward,* is about responsibility and service. The term *steward* means there is a master. What we are really talking about in stewardship is the human side of the lordship equation. God's side is Lord; our side is steward.

So should we make money the primary focus of stewardship or can we say that stewardship is integration of the Lordship of Jesus Christ into every area of life? What area of your life would you like to shut God out of?

There is a basic law of physics and of human dynamics: For every action there is an equal and opposite reaction. And this applies when the preacher mentions stewardship. You feel pressured, so you naturally resist and push back. Which means in order to get more money, he has to push harder, which means you resist harder. Right? That's what happens when we make stewardship only about money.

OF COURSE, WHEN I SAY THE WORD STEWARDSHIP THE FIRST THING THAT COMES TO MIND IS MONEY.

What we really want to look at is how God can be Lord of every part of our lives, everything we are individually and as a church. I hope that begins to open up a new dimension of what stewardship is all about.

Values today

As background to our exploration of stewardship, let us consider some of the key values we face in many cultures of the world today:

1. The value of independence. People want to be on their own and want to survive on their own, not dependent on anyone else. This focus on not needing each other has broken down the extended family and even the nuclear family, and family bonds aren't as strong as they once were.

2. An attitude of self-reliance. Many people say, "I can do it by myself, I don't need anybody else."

3. Accomplishment is emphasized, which is really a focus on what we can do for ourselves.

4. Status comes with focusing on the importance of position, power, authority and money.

5. Power. Everybody wants more power, especially when we feel powerless against so many things in our society.

These values are both symptoms of and contributors to some of the big trends of our time, such as secularism, materialism, relativism, increasing polarization and globalization.

And it doesn't take too much reflection to recognize that some of these values have had an impact in the church. But if we are going to do anything about it, only a biblical lifestyle or a biblical vision of Christianity can lead us back to a Christian lifestyle.

DISCIPLESHIP

Chapter 2

When you hear the word *Christian*, what comes to mind?" What is one of the most common descriptions or definitions of the word Christian? How would you define Christian? Are you a Christian? Are you Christ-like?

When I have asked these questions in seminars, usually almost everyone raises their hand saying they are Christians. But when I ask how many are Christ-like, only a few hands go up. There is a gap between the two because we allow culture to shape and redefine Christianity to the point where in many places in the world today Christianity is virtually synonymous with the culture around us.

Conversation on a plane

Sometime ago, I was flying home to where I was then living, connecting from Calgary to Denver and then to Baltimore Washington Airport. On the flight from Calgary to Denver, I was upgraded to first class. That doesn't happen to me often but I think God had a reason on this trip.

I ended up sitting beside a company executive from a Canadian oil company. We got chatting and I asked him who he was and what he did, and he asked me who I was and what I did.

"Stewardship? Director of stewardship of the Seventh Day Adventist Church?" he repeated what I had told him as question. "What do you do?"

"Well I travel all over the world training leaders and church members—but primarily pastors and church leaders—in the principles of radical Christianity," I explained.

"BUT LET ME ASK YOU A QUESTION: WHAT DIFFERENCE DOES THEIR CHRISTIANITY MAKE IN THEIR EVERYDAY LIFE?"

He still was looking for more explanation, so I said, "I talk about what it means to really be a Christian."

"I was born and raised as a Roman Catholic and I am really not a practicing Roman Catholic today," he said. "I would like to know a little more of what you are talking about here."

"Well," I said, "let's look at it this way. If I were to walk down the streets of Calgary and ask the average pedestrian there, 'Are you a Christian?' what would they say?"

"Most of them will say, 'Of course,'" he suggested.

"In fact, some of them will be insulted that I would even ask, wouldn't they?" I said. "But let me ask you a question: what difference does their Christianity make in their everyday life?"

"Absolutely none," he said without hesitation.

"That's my point," I said. "Because it's really not Christianity if it isn't making a difference in our lives. If we are no different from the rest of the culture around us, then are we really Christians? So what we are talking about is a radical Christianity that believes God can make a difference in our daily lives."

"I bet you find people hungry for that all over the world," he said.

"I do," I assured him.

"I bet you find your greater hunger among lay members than you do among the clergy," was his next suggestion—and I had to agree.

Comparison game

We have allowed culture to shape and redefine our Christianity. We come to a place where we accept mediocrity as the normal, rather than the close fellowship with God for which we were created and which is our true normal. We experience the gradual drift or erosion of values in norms and practices in the church, gradually becoming more and more like the world around us.

WE ACCEPT MEDIOCRITY AS NORMAL, RATHER THAN THE CLOSE FELLOWSHIP WITH GOD FOR WHICH WE WERE CREATED AND WHICH IS OUR TRUE NORMAL

Over time, we come to consider biblical expectations as unrealistic. We tell ourselves, *Surely what God expected of Paul, Enoch and Moses, He doesn't expect of me. I mean, I live in the 21st century and society has changed. Surely he does not expect that kind of relationship with me, does He?* Yes, He does.

But in the depths of our hearts, how many of us really feel like we could walk beside Enoch or David, Paul or Peter and be considered normal among them? Or have we somehow allowed our definitions to shift to the point where we are comfortable with not quite that high an expectation.

> **HOW MANY OF US REALLY FEEL LIKE WE COULD WALK BESIDE ENOCH OR DAVID, PAUL OR PETER AND BE CONSIDERED NORMAL AMONG THEM?**

We naturally tend to measure ourselves by each other. And we do much of this in the church, constantly looking for the faults of each other. It's so common because our assurance comes on the level of our behavior. I look at myself and I see my problem, so the only way I can feel good about myself is if I am a little bit better than someone else. So when I look at you I don't look for your good points, I look for your problems. In this twisted reasoning, your good points make me feel worse but your problems make me feel better about myself.

Christ-like?

God loves us unconditionally and there is nothing we can do to make Him love us more or that will make Him love us less. Then why do so many of us still tell our children, "You better be good because if you are not good, Jesus won't love you"? I have heard it all over the world. If a child grows up hearing that, which are they going to believe— God's unconditional love or God's love depending on their behavior? Here our theory and our practice begin to separate.

BEING
JUST A
LITTLE
BIT
CHRISTIAN
IS NO MORE
POSSIBLE
THAN BEING
JUST A
LITTLE BIT
PREGNANT.

But is it possible to be a little bit Christian? Or does being a little bit Christian imply that we are a great deal pagan? There is no middle ground. Being just a little bit Christian is no more possible than a woman being just a little bit pregnant. It just doesn't happen. She either is or isn't. There is a nine-month process of development before birth takes place but during that nine months, everything is changing. It is all or nothing.

It is the same way with being a Christian. Didn't Paul say if any man be in Christ he is a new creation—"They are not the same anymore, for the old life is gone. A new life has begun!" (2 Corinthians 5:17)?

At the beginning of this chapter, I asked, "Are you Christ-like?" This is a question many Christians struggle to answer. But when we accept Jesus, He gives to us His salvation and righteousness. And one of the common metaphors used in the Bible to describe this gift is a robe of righteousness (see, for example, Job 29:14, Isaiah 61:10 and Matthew 22:2-14). He does not give us just part of the robe. The moment we accept Jesus we are fully clothed in a robe of His righteousness that covers all of us.

So who knows the real you? You, when you look in the mirror, or God? Your neighbor or God? God says you are like Christ. We think we know ourselves but what we know is the old self without Christ. Christ's righteousness does not mean I have become like him because I have reached a level of performance, it means He has covered me and I am like Him because I have Christ and the process of becoming like Him has begun. But I am like Him when I am in Him.

May I suggest that robe of righteousness is also like a portable dry cleaning unit. It doesn't just cover, it also cleanses. John wrote, "If we confess our sins to him, he is faithful and just to forgive us and to cleanse us from every wrong" (1 John 1:9).

Deceptions

We have accepted two deceptions of the devil.

The first is he has made us think it is difficult to live the Christian life. We are told it is going to be a hard road, that if we survive it at all, it will be by the skin of our teeth. That is an absolute falsehood.

The easiest thing in the world to do is to live the Christian life. Not because there are no problems, difficulties or challenges but because God has provided His strength and power to help us.

Peter put it like this: "As we know Jesus better, his divine power gives us everything we need for living a godly life. He has called us to receive his own glory and goodness! And by that same mighty power, he has given us all of his rich and wonderful promises. He has promised that you will escape the decadence all around you caused by evil desires and that you will share in his divine nature" (2 Peter 1:3, 4).

If I have to dig a big hole for a house foundation and all you give me is a shovel, that is going to be a big job. But if you come along with a large bulldozer, a backhoe and front loader, it's going to be an easy job.

THE POWER AND THE EQUIPMENT AVAILABLE TO DO THE JOB MAKE THE DIFFERENCE.

The power and the equipment available to do the job make the difference. Peter says God's divine power has given us everything we need for life. In other words, living the Christian life is easy because of the source of power available to us. That's why Paul can say, "For I can do everything with the help of Christ who gives me the strength I need" (Philippians 4:13).

The other deception is the idea that it is easy to become a Christian. All you have to do is say, "I accept Jesus," we are sometimes told. This is true of accepting the gift of salvation but to become a Christian and live as a disciple of Jesus is not something to be taken lightly. The toughest thing you will ever do is become a Christian, because to become a Christian you have to die. Too many of us want the benefits of Christianity without dying. We want to decide where we have the robe or don't—but you can't have a partial robe.

Holiness for beginners

Similar to our hesitation in describing ourselves as Christ-like is our reaction to holiness. Maybe we misunderstand holy. Maybe part of the problem is that we have grown up in the world that considers holy as being so good that we don't need outside help. In order to be a saint, we are told, we have to be like Mother Theresa, who gave her entire life in ministry to the poorest of the poor to the point where her church is ready to canonize her as a saint.

But no church can make a person a saint, only God can make a saint. When is the last time you read First Corinthians? We would not consider those people very saintly. There were all kinds of problems in that church. But Paul still calls them saints.

So what makes a saint? Three words in the English—*saint* is the noun, *sanctify* is a verb, *holy* is the adjective—go back to two basis words, one in Greek and one in Hebrew.

BUT THE GROUND ITSELF WASN'T HOLY, RATHER THE PRESENCE OF GOD MADE IT HOLY.

Moses is looking after the sheep in the desert and sees a burning bush in the distance. His curiosity overwhelms him. He comes up to that bush and a voice speaks to him and says, "Take off your sandals, for you are standing on holy ground" (Exodus 3:5).

But the ground itself wasn't holy, rather the presence of God made it holy. That's the only thing that can make anything holy. And if God is with you and in you, doesn't that make you holy?

Holiness is not based on what you do. It is based on Who is with you.

• And Jesus said, "And be sure of this: I am with you always, even to the end of the age" (Matthew 28:20).

• And Paul wrote, "When I think of the wisdom and scope of God's plan, I fall to my knees and pray to the Father, the Creator of everything in heaven and on earth. I pray that from his glorious, unlimited resources he will give you mighty inner strength through his Holy Spirit. And I pray that Christ will be more and more at home in your hearts as you trust in him" (Ephesians 3:14-17).

• Paul also wrote, "For in Christ the fullness of God lives in a human body, and you are complete through your union with Christ" (Colossians 2:9, 10).

• When Jesus gave the promise of the Holy Spirit to His disciples, He said, "On that day, you will realize that I am in my Father, and you are in me, and I am in you" (John 14:20, NIV).

With God dwelling in us and with us, aren't we saints? The issue for holiness and sainthood is not how good am I but have I accepted the living presence of Jesus Christ.

Secular life?

One of the strange habits we have is describing non-church activities as secular. But with the understanding we have of God's presence, can a Christian have a secular life?

If a Christian is a Christian, he or she has God with them wherever they go. Therefore, every part of our life is sanctified by God's presence.

At times, as a church, we have told our young people to stay out of the movie theaters, because "if you go in there, God stays outside." But the reality that should really influence our entertainment choices is the realization that when we are watching that television program, movie or online video clip, God is beside us. So how comfortable are you in that activity with God beside you?

Describing a disciple

Biblical Christianity is dynamic. It is focused on Christ. It is committed 100 per cent. It is passionate. It is transformational. It is fruitful. It is peaceful and it is loving and accepting. God makes us stewards or partners with Him—and that's a different way of living.

A disciple is one who walks with, learns from and lives in submission to a master in order to become like the master. There are five biblical descriptions of discipleship that need our attention:

1. A disciple passionately loves Jesus Christ.

Jesus said, "Love me with all your heart, mind, soul and strength. Let me be the consuming passion of your life" (see Mark 12:30). You have been His consuming passion for the entire history of this earth and

He simply says, "Love me like I love you." A disciple passionately loves Jesus Christ first.

2. A disciple maintains intimacy with God through a daily devotional life.

In any relationship, the level of passion is in direct proportion to the level of intimacy. If you want more passion for God, the intimacy with God has to grow.

3. The disciple integrates Christ into every area of life.

A husband and wife don't become fully intimate until they are also friends, which comes from sharing and growing in everyday life.

4. The disciple makes Christ the priority in every decision.

Decisions like where I live, what I drive, what I wear, everything, must have Christ as the priority. Standards of behavior are useless if this internal relationship is not dealt with. Only the living presence of Christ can lead a person to make the prior decision they need to make.

5. A disciple actively shares Christ with those around him or her.

Christian researcher George Barna has spent time exploring what he describes as "transient Christianity" in our world today. He suggests that less than half those who attend Christian churches are really Christians. And reflecting on the biblical descriptions of discipleship perhaps even fewer of our members are truly disciples.

A DISCIPLE IS ONE WHO WALKS WITH, LEARNS FROM AND LIVES IN SUBMISSION TO A MASTER IN ORDER TO BECOME LIKE THE MASTER.

STORY
Chapter 3

When we start to think about where we are as a church and as Christians, most of us have to face the reality that we are a long way from where we would like to be. But there is a greater reality. We need to learn to see things as God might see them.

God created

It begins at Creation. God steps out on space and creates this world. He speaks and it comes to be. By the power of His voice, light appears and waters are separated. Land masses appear, plants appear. Fish swim through the waters. Birds fly through the air. Animals walk on the land. All by the power of His voice.

He could have spoken one more time, and Adam and Eve would have walked on the land. But the picture is radically different. God wants to become intimately involved in the creation of humanity.

God says to Themselves—bad grammar but good theology—"Let us make people in our image" (Genesis 1:26). Perhaps we can imagine God stooping beside the river, gathering the soil and clay, putting it together and beginning to shape it in His own image.

GOD WANTS TO BECOME INTIMATELY INVOLVED IN THE CREATION OF HUMANITY.

Here in the creation story we discover the foundational principles of stewardship and of the Christian walk with God. God shared His image with humanity and we were created for the purpose of reflecting His image throughout eternity.

The image of God

The first principle tells us that the process of redemption has the restoration of the image of God in humankind as one of its goals.

Picture with me the scene of the Creator God shaping that clay with His hands. I have often asked myself, "How did He do what He did?" Did he start with the skin of the back, then the backbone, the ribs, connecting all the bones, one bone connected to the next bone, then take the organs and shape them and put them each in its place and then begin to apply the tendons, muscles and finally the flesh, the skin, the hair? Or did He simply form the exterior with His hand and allow the breath of His mouth to shape the interior?

PICTURE WITH ME THE SCENE OF THE CREATOR GOD SHAPING THAT CLAY WITH HIS HANDS.

I don't know. But one day I want to find out.

When I get to heaven, I want to ask God to play this back on the giant screen. Surely God can replay the creation story for us, however He did it.

In my imagination, I can picture Him working but standing up from time to time, like any artist would, leaning from one side to the other, seeing how it looks, bending down to make a few more adjustments.

Some time ago, I was in the city of Florence, Italy. When I walked into the plaza in front of the old Palace, there on the corner was a reproduction of Michaelangelo's *David*. The original is in the museum to protect it from the elements and vandals. As I stood looking at that sculpture, which is probably the most famous sculpture in all the world, I saw its perfect symmetry and its beauty and I couldn't help but think, *That can't begin to compare with what God must have done.* When God is finished shaping that clay into the form that would become Adam, it must be perfect. But it is still just a lump of clay.

Intimacy with God

God could have said, "Live"—and in an instant that lump of clay would have jumped to his feet and walked around. But what an incredible act of intimacy.

We see this Creator God bending over one more time, placing His lips over the nostril and lips of clay and breathing in the breath of life and man becomes a living being.

Do you realize what happened in that instant?

Faster than we could explain or describe, what was clay becomes living flesh.

What was clay becomes bronchial tubes, taking the oxygen down into the lungs.

What was clay becomes those fine alveoli, fragile air sacs where the exchange of gasses between the air and the blood takes place.

What was clay becomes veins and arteries.

What was clay becomes blood flowing through.

What was clay becomes a heart, pumping 60 to 80 times a minute on average, taking life and nutrition to the rest of the body.

What was clay becomes living bone and tissue, muscle and flesh.

What was clay becomes a nervous system, shaping the signals and impulses back and forth throughout the body.

What was clay becomes the human brain with all its incredible capacity and functions.

And as that life reaches those brain cells, the eyelids flicker open and the first bit of information to register on the human brain is a picture of the face of the Creator God, lifting from the intimacy of a kiss of life.

Can you imagine that first conversation?

"Excuse me God, who are you?"

"Who am I? I'm God the Creator. And you, Adam, are the first man. I have just finished shaping you with My hands and breathing into you the

"I CREATED YOU THROUGH AN ACT OF INTIMACY BECAUSE I WANT TO BE FRIENDS WITH YOU THROUGHOUT ETERNITY."

breath of life. You look at Me and you see a little bit of yourself, where I have shared My image with you. I have created you in My likeness."

"But Adam, I have also shared intimacy with you. I created you through an act of intimacy because I want to be friends with you throughout eternity."

You and I were created for friendship with God. It is normal to live in step with God.

As He looked down through the ages of eternity, God could not imagine an eternity without us and He created us for that friendship. And stewardship must have the restoration of that intimacy as one of its foundational principles.

Shared governance

I can also imagine that conversation going on as God turns to Adam and He says, "Do you see this beautiful world I have created for you? You see this beautiful garden called Eden; I have created it for you. It is My world and My garden but I am willing to share their governance with you. I will give you dominion over this world and I will make you My representative, My agent, managing My affairs on earth."

HE ALLOWS A HUMAN BEING TO BECOME HIS AGENT IN MANAGING HIS AFFAIRS ON EARTH.

Not only does God share image with us and share intimacy with us, the third principle of stewardship is shared governance. He allows a human being to become His agent in managing His affairs on earth.

Interdependence

If God continued with one more principle, He would have said to Adam, "In order to manage My affairs on earth and share My governance, you must realize you are totally dependant on Me and I am dependant on you."

For some reason, God chose to be dependant on humanity. It is hard for me to imagine that God would depend on me for anything, not because He had to but because He chose to.

Creation lost

From Creation come these first four principles of stewardship and a daily Christian life:

• God shares His image with us and we are created to share that image throughout eternity.

• He shares His intimacy with us for we are to be friends with God.

• He shares His governance with us. We are to be His agents.

• And He shares His dependence or interdependence with us.

We are to work hand in hand with Him as partners with God. But we didn't stay there. With one simple act, the human race became a fallen race. These four foundational principles of life are totally destroyed and turned upside down by sin.

What was shared image became a sinful nature. What was shared intimacy became a shattered union. What was shared governance became a slavery to sin. And what was shared dependence or interdependence became a false independence.

But God didn't leave us there. When we could no longer come to Him, He came to us and we are redeemed as we look to God, and realize who He is and what He has done.

WHEN WE COULD NO LONGER COME TO HIM, HE CAME TO US.

• When we can no longer share His image because of sin, He comes and shares with us the likeness of our sinful flesh, yet without sin. Paul says He made Him to be sin for us (see 2 Corinthians 5:21).

- When we could no longer share His governance because we were in slavery to sin, He came and redeemed us and turned us from slaves of sin to slaves of God (see Romans 6).

- When sin replaced our dependence on Him with a false independence, He came and modelled a total dependence on the Father. Over and over in the Book of John, Jesus said that "I assure you, the Son can do nothing by himself" (John 5:19; see also John 8:28). And in following Him, we are restored to total dependence on and interdependence with God.

- But He didn't just redeem us. He also has adopted us as His children. He restores us to our status in Him and we share a deeper intimacy with Him. Jesus said, "I no longer call you servants, because a master doesn't confide in his servants. Now you are my friends, since I have told you everything the Father told me" (John 15:15).

Called to more

The restoration of this relationship is a call to a more radical obedience. A slave obeys because he has to and a child obeys only as long as he has to but a friend obeys because he or she wants to.

But it doesn't stop there because God also promises to enthrone us. Remember the promise to the church in Laodicea: " I will invite everyone who is victorious to sit with me on my throne, just as I was victorious and sat with my Father on his throne" (Revelation 3:21).

Victory to overcome comes in Jesus Christ through His power and His victory on Calvary

A SLAVE OBEYS BECAUSE HE HAS TO AND A CHILD OBEYS ONLY AS LONG AS HE HAS TO BUT A FRIEND OBEYS BECAUSE HE OR SHE WANTS TO.

when we accept Him. So the moment I accept Jesus Christ as Savior, that moment I am a conqueror and overcomer. And in that moment I am enthroned with God and have the privilege of sitting with God.

A royal priesthood

In Revelation 1:6, we are told that Jesus "has made us his Kingdom and his priests who serve before God his Father." In 1 Peter 2:5, we are described as "God's holy priests." In verse 9, Peter says, "You are a kingdom of priests." But what do these statements really mean?

In the patriarchal system, the patriarch of the family functioned as priest and king. That is the situation of Melchizedek, described as "the king of Salem and a priest of God Most High" (Genesis 14:18).

That combination continues until we come down to God's people. Moses and Aaron separate the two roles, kingly and priestly roles. They are rarely combined except in a couple of judges like Eli and Samuel and once a king was selected, it was a permanent separation until we come to Jesus, who was the priest-king and sacrifice on Calvary.

THE CHRISTIAN BEGINS LIFE FROM THE VERY THRONE OF GOD.

According to the Bible texts we have looked at, you and I are priests after the order of Jesus Christ, who is the priest after the order of Melchizedek. We are a royal priesthood.

Ephesians 1:19-21 describes God's power resurrecting Jesus Christ and seating Him at His right hand in heavenly places. In the next chapter (see Ephesians 2:6), Paul says that in Christ you have been raised and seated with Him in heavenly places. In other words, the Christian begins life from the very throne of God. And a person on the throne has all the power of the throne. All of the power of God is available to you to live every day in Him.

Is it any wonder that James can say, "So humble yourselves before

God. Resist the Devil, and he will flee from you" (James 4:7)? He has no other choice. When you resist him in Christ, the power that overcame him on Calvary is working in you to resist him and drive him away. Is it any wonder that Peter wrote, "As we know Jesus better, his divine power gives us everything we need for living a godly life" (2 Peter 1:3)?

More closely united to God

This is a picture of where Christian life begins. We are not merely redeemed, trying to make it to the throne. We start life as Christians from the very throne of God.

Can you think of any greater vision than to realize who we are in Jesus Christ? Holy, transformed, clothed in His righteousness, seated on His throne, co-heirs with Christ. That excites me.

It reminds me of the devil's first deception in this world. If you eat of this tree, he said, "you will become just like God" (Genesis 3:5).

But they shared His image. They shared intimacy with Him. They shared his governance. They were interdependent with Him. The only thing they didn't have was the ability to be God in themselves— Lucifer always offers a counterfeit substitute. He wanted to be on God's throne. It must be galling to him when he thinks of where the Christian is in Christ, exactly where he wanted to be.

"BY HIS LIFE AND HIS DEATH, CHRIST HAS ACHIEVED EVEN MORE THAN RECOVERY FROM THE RUIN WROUGHT THROUGH SIN."

Remarkably, *The Desire of Ages* tells us that because of sin and the plan of redemption, we will be closer to God than if we had never sinned: "By His life and His death, Christ has achieved even more than recovery from the ruin wrought through sin. . . . In Christ, we become more closely united to God than if we had never fallen" (page 25). Because of what God has done for us, we can know the fullness of God's love and redemption.

GOD

Chapter 4

It's amazing what happens when we begin to catch a vision of who God is and who we are. That's where Christian stewardship really begins.

It starts with recognizing who God is and learning to let God be God, because stewardship is based on who God is.

But what does it mean for God to be God?

We cannot explore it all because we would never run out of material to cover. Throughout eternity we will be exploring the wonder of God. But let's explore a little.

Incomparable

First of all, God is incomparable. No one can compare or compete with Him.

Think about it: Who else could have created life?

In Central America where I grew up, we had a tree called the devil's tree. I'm sure you have eaten its fruit or its nut at least as a cashew nut. The reason they call it the devil's tree is they say that when God finished creation the devil said, "I can create something, too." So he created this beautiful tree with a beautiful fruit. It is bright orange when its ripe and highly acidic. But the story goes, he forgot the seed and so he had to put it on the outside of the fruit. And so to this day, the cashew nut hangs on the end of the fruit outside.

NO ONE CAN COMPARE OR COMPETE WITH HIM.

Of course, that is just folklore but it points out that nobody can compare with our God. He is beyond comparison and yet He has chosen to deal with us.

Transcendent

The second aspect of Him being creator is He is transcendent. He is far beyond this and all that we know. He is a God who can deal with issues you and I cannot even begin to comprehend.

Let me give you one example that absolutely boggles my mind. Remember the story of King Hezekiah in 2 Kings 20:1-11. He falls sick, he prays, the prophet comes and says, "You are going to die."

Hezekiah prays again, and the prophet returns and says, "OK, God will heal you."

"How do I know?" asks Hezekiah.

"He will give you a sign," replies the prophet. "Do you want the sun dial to move forward 10 degrees or back 10 degrees?"

"Everybody knows the sun dial is going to move forward 10 degrees," says Hezekiah. "So let's turn it back 10."

God is pretty busy for this moment. Do you realize everything He has to do to stop the world in its rotation on its axis, back it up 10 degrees and restart it?

If you know anything about physics, you would understand that action of stopping, reversing and restarting should have torn asunder the tectonic plates of this planet. Continents should have shifted in their place. There should have been massive earthquakes destroying everything in this world and massive tidal waves sweeping across the land,

GOD KEPT IT ALL IN BALANCE WITH THE TOUCH OF ONE FINGER— JUST TO STRENGTHEN THE WEAK FAITH OF A SINFUL KING.

destroying all life.

But God kept it all in balance with the touch of one finger—just to strengthen the weak faith of a sinful king. It is hard to understand a God with that kind of capability.

Immanent

But God is not only transcendent, He is also immanent. This is a theological and technical term used to describe God, meaning He is

intimately involved in our lives. He is there with us. His name is Immanuel— "God with us" (see Matthew 1:23). Think about how far that goes. At one moment in time, God became one fertilized ovum in the womb of a young woman named Mary. For a moment in time, God—all the fullness of God that dwells in Christ in bodily form—is now one fertilized cell that a moment later becomes two, then four, then eight, then 16, then 32, then 64, and on and on until that duplication begins to differentiate. Blood vessels appear and a tiny pumping heart develops, then arms and fingers and toes and head and ears, all begin to appear as God chooses to become the God-man. "God with us": the transcendent God who controls the universe, intimately involved, immanently present with us.

Creative

When we see God as Creator, of course we also recognize that God is creative.

I have visited Australia a number of times and I have enjoyed coming to know a little about that incredible continent. It seems like God dealt with Australia specially when He got through creating all the rest of the world.

What kind of God would create a platypus? It is as if He had a bunch of left over parts that He just stuck together. A fur-bearing animal that suckles its young and lays eggs. It has a duck bill and the males have a poison gland for defence. It's amazing. And then there are animals like koalas and kangaroos.

You know your creativity comes from God. Think of the creative gifts expressed or represented among your group of friends. Then recognize that this is just a sampling of God's creative ability.

Sovereign

God is also sovereign. He is free, autonomous. He is the God of the universe, which makes it even more amazing that He would stop and think about us. The Lord God, Who is, Who was and Who is to come, Who has no beginning or end.

How do we comprehend eternity and God's sovereignty in the scope of eternity? I can try to understand life without end. I have it now in Christ. But I cannot comprehend life without beginning. What was there before that? Our logic breaks down. And yet God was there.

As far back as you can begin to imagine, God was there and He was Sovereign. God is Savior. God is involved. The Father is intimately involved as He gives His son. In a sense, God the Father gives more than does the Son, for He gives His Son. Those of us who are parents can understand that would be a greater sacrifice than to give ourselves. And the Holy Spirit is also

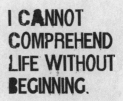

I CANNOT COMPREHEND LIFE WITHOUT BEGINNING.

involved in that process. The Son becomes human to live and die with us—and He is coming back to rule and be with us forever.

This sovereignty also applies to the things of this world. God is owner of all: "For all the animals of the forest are mine, and I own the cattle on a thousand hills," says God in Psalm 50:10.

So why do we so arrogantly think we are owner of anything? We say, "*My* car, *my* house, *my* family, *my* church." But God reminds us that He owns it all.

Love

God is also love. 1 John 4:7,8 helps us realize that each of his actions originates from and is based on love. Romans 5:8 points that out. But God is love. Everything about Him comes from a God of Love.

I love the "Conflict of the Ages" series. This epic re-telling of the history of humanity begins with the book *Patriarchs and Prophets*. What are the first words in *Patriarchs and Prophets*? "God is Love."

THE WHOLE PROCESS OF REDEMPTION IS TO RE-ESTABLISH, FOR ALL ETERNITY AND ALL THE UNIVERSE, THE FACT THAT GOD IS LOVE.

And what are the final words in the concluding book of the series, *The Great Controversy*? Again, "God is Love."

The whole process of redemption is to re-establish, for all eternity and all the universe, the fact that God is Love. He needs to express Himself because love without expression is meaningless. Creation is a manifestation of His love. And unselfish love belongs to Him and keeps stewardship from becoming slavery.

It's a point worth remembering: Stewardship without a love relationship with God is nothing more than spiritual slavery.

Present

And God is present. He wants to be with us through every part of our lives.

It is hard for me to imagine that God would want to be with me. There are times

IT IS HARD FOR ME TO IMAGINE THAT GOD WOULD WANT TO BE WITH ME.

when it embarrasses me. There are time it shames me. But it always overwhelms me.

In this truth we can catch a glimpse of the reason for our existence as human beings:

1. To be an object of God's love.

2. To be a vehicle of God's love to the world around us.

3. To manifest God's love to the world and

to the universe.

I love the verse in Zephaniah 3:17 that describes God in this way: "For the Lord your God has arrived to live among you. He is a mighty savior. He will rejoice over you with great gladness. With his love, he will calm all your fears. He will exult over you by singing a happy song."

Imagine God in Heaven stepping down from His throne, raising His hand and stopping the angel choirs. He says, "Stop, it's My turn to sing. Down there is a group of people who are gathering together to study about Me. It brings joy to my heart and I can't help but sing. I want to rejoice over them with singing."

And a deep wondrous voice like the sound of many waters begins to sing a song of joy over His re-creation, over us. Then the angel choirs join in with the background harmonies and it is a song of redemption and joy over us in heaven, in God's heart.

And in different ways, we are called to manifest and express this love of God in the world.

Judgment: good news

When we recognize we are to vindicate God's love and justice, we gain a better picture of what the judgment is all about. At times, we have become lost in the issue of the investigative judgment. We have used it to scare people into making decisions. We have argued about whether it is biblical or not.

But Daniel 7—the chapter on the judgment—tells us that the judgment does four wonderful things. There are four ways of answering the four issues of the challenge to God in His government that is at the heart of the "Great Controversy":

1. The first thing that judgment does is vindicate God. At the close of that judgment, every knee bows to worship God because God has been vindicated before the universe.

2. The judgment vindicates Christ and gives Him the kingdom. Christ's position in heaven was questioned by Lucifer but He has overcome this challenge.

3. The judgment vindicates the saints. God's people have judgment pronounced in their favor and they receive the kingdom.

4. The judgment demonstrates God's right to destroy sin and sinners. The little horn, as the representative of sin, is cast in the fire and destroyed. The issue of God's character and His government is resolved on the universal scale.

Ephesians 3:10 says, "God's purpose was to show his wisdom in all its rich variety to all the rulers and authorities in the heavenly realms." We vindicate God's character. That is part of our reason for existence. In us, God finds character witnesses to testify before Him and in His favor before the universe.

So why should I fear the judgment? I am standing there to talk about Him.

Whose robe am I wearing? His robe.

Who is my judge? Christ is.

Who is my advocate? Christ is.

Who has already paid the price of sin? Christ has.

What do I have to be afraid of? As 1 John 4:17 puts it, "we will not be afraid on the day of judgment, but we can face him with confidence."

Imagine . . .

So what would happen if what we have considered here became reality in our hearts and minds, if we really began to live from the perspective of who God is and who we are in Him?
Letting God be God and recognizing Him for Who and What He truly is must transform us, our lives, our attitudes and our confidence.

When Jesus' disciples Peter and John healed a lame man, they were brought before the Sanhedrin—the religious authority of the day—to examine their actions and probably to try to intimidate them into being quiet about Jesus. But it seems it was the religious leaders who were overwhelmed: "The members of the council were amazed when they saw the boldness of Peter and John, for they could see that they were ordinary men who had had no special training. They also recognized them as men who had been with Jesus" (Acts 4:13).

When we confront these realities of God we can have that same kind of transformation and confidence.

LETTING GOD BE GOD AND RECOGNIZING HIM FOR WHO AND WHAT HE TRULY IS MUST TRANSFORM US.

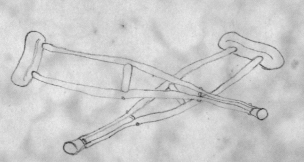

STEWARDSHIP

Chapter 5

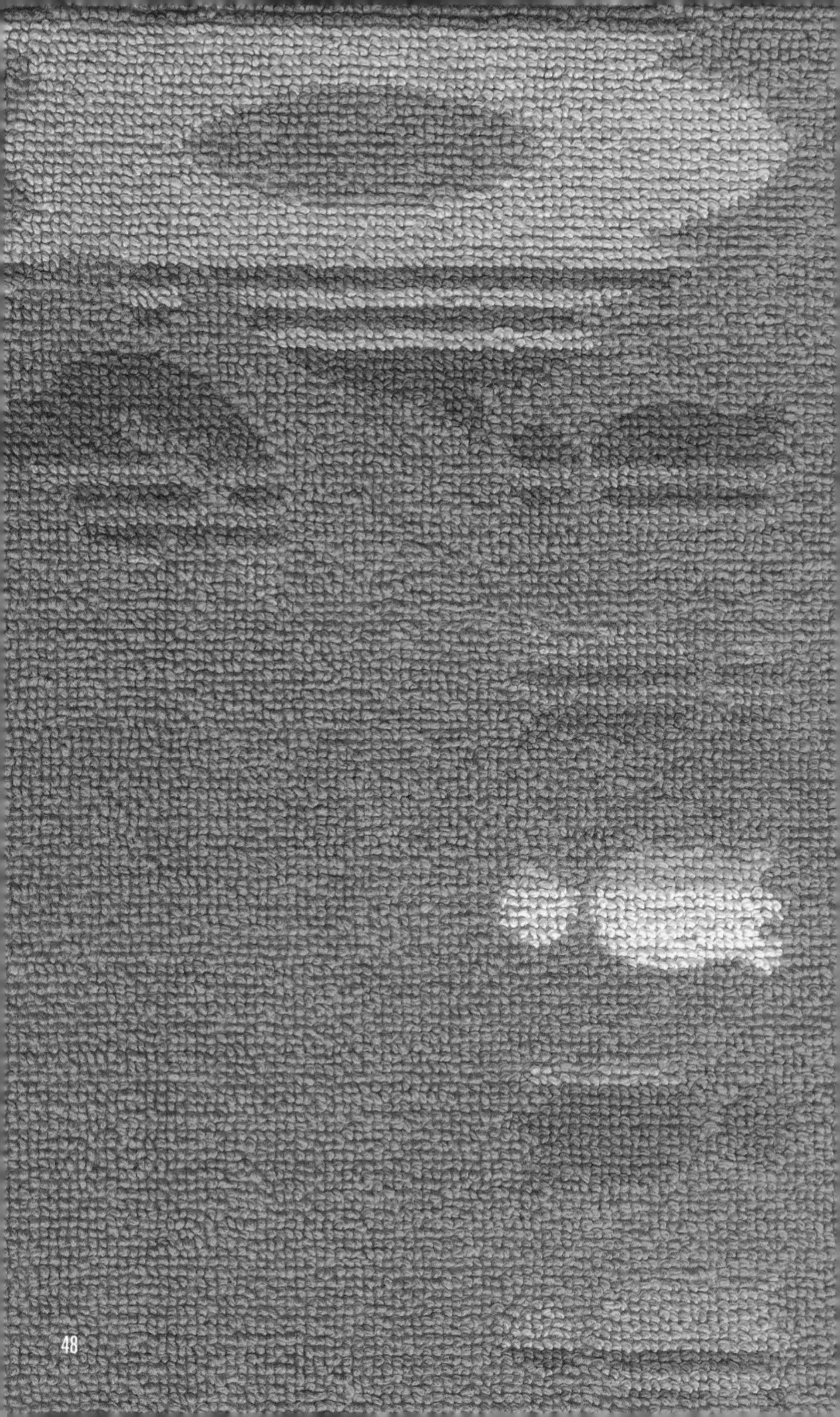

What we have been talking about is not just idealism. God doesn't give us a picture of who we are without assuring us He can make it happen. It will only happen as He becomes Lord of every part of our lives and we realize this is who we already are in Christ. Our history and our life change the moment we accept Christ.

Writing in Romans 5, Paul ends with that incredible promise, "God's law was given so that all people could see how sinful they were. But as people sinned more and more, God's wonderful kindness became more abundant" (Romans 5:20). Paul knows there are some narrowed-minded people, who are going to have the thought, *I want more grace, I will go out and sin a little more.*

Paul says, "Well then, should we keep on sinning so that God can show us more and more kindness and forgiveness? Of course not! Since we have died to sin, how can we continue to live in it?" (Romans 6:1, 2). Then his argument is, "Have you forgotten that when we became Christians and were baptized to become one with Christ Jesus, we died with him? . . . Now we also may live new lives" (Romans 6:3, 4).

He gets down to verse 11: "So you should consider yourselves dead to sin and able to live for the glory of God through Christ Jesus." In verse 14, he continues, "Sin is no longer your master, for you are no longer subject to the law, which enslaves you to sin. Instead, you are free by God's grace."

OUR HISTORY AND OUR LIFE CHANGE THE MOMENT WE ACCEPT CHRIST.

When we accept Christ, we are part of a new kingdom, a new reality. We are part of his family. We are not trying to get there or work our way to the kingdom. We are not trying to earn the throne. We are on the throne. We are in Christ. The rest of life simply becomes living that out, which is what stewardship is all about.

But we need to redefine stewardship. So let's look at some basic biblical presuppositions that form the foundation for the lordship relationship of Jesus Christ.

Presupposition 1: A personal God

God is a personal God, intimately involved in every part of our lives. 1 Corinthians 6:19, 20 is an interesting text in this regard: "Or don't you know that your body is the temple of the Holy Spirit, who lives in you and was given to you by God? You do not belong to yourself, for God bought you with a high price. So you must honor God with your body."

We use these verses as an argument for healthful living totally out of context. The principle applies but the passage deals with fornication. We are often tempted to tell people to clean up their lives so God can

GOD SAYS, "CLEAN UP YOUR LIFE BECAUSE I AM ALREADY WITH YOU AND IN YOU."

live in them. But Paul says something radically different. He says, "Don't unite yourself with a prostitute because you are one with God."

We say, "Clean up your life to be good enough for God."

God says, "Clean up your life because I am already with you and in you."

His personal involvement in our lives is not dependent on our behavior. Rather, our behavior is dependent on His personal involvement. The motivation for changing is that He has already entered our lives. Without Him, we have no desire to change.

Presupposition 2: God is in control

God is in control, guiding the history and affairs of this world and its people.

Some years ago, I was teaching this in a seminar in Europe. One of the more influential pastors in the group stood up and challenged what I was saying.

"I can't believe that you from the General Conference would come and teach this kind of childish scribble that God is in control," he said. "If God is in control how do you explain the Holocaust? How do you explain the thousands and thousands that were killed in Rwanda?"

The Bible doesn't explain all these tragedies, outrages and disappointments but part of the issue is learning to deal with the mystery of God, learning to let God be God even when we don't understand all the issues.

But the Bible clearly states that God is in control. Paul went so far as to say that He sets up and takes down kings (see Romans 13)—and he was talking about the Roman Emperor!

Presupposition 3: God is owner of all

As Creator and Redeemer, God is owner of all. Thus, He is Provider of all.

If God owns everything, why do you and I worry about anything? Jesus said, "So don't worry about having enough food or drink or clothing. Why be like the pagans who are so deeply concerned about these things? Your heavenly Father already knows all your needs, and he will give you all you need from day to day if you live for him and make the Kingdom of God your primary concern" (Matthew 6:31-33).

I AM CLAIMING TO BE THE ONE WHO HAS TO BE IN CONTROL OF THINGS.

In other words, when I worry, I am claiming to be owner. I am claiming to be the one who has to be in control of things. I am trying to be my own god.

If God is really God, owner of everything, He provides everything we need. And that is what Peter said, "His divine power gives us everything we need for living a godly life. He has called us to receive his own glory and goodness!" (2 Peter 1:3). That includes all of life.

Presupposition 4: God is in control of His church

God is in direct control of His church, while allowing room for human decisions.

This one is a little tougher for me. I have wrestled with God over this one. At one time when I was wrestling with these questions, I had little problem concluding that the church is God's and that God is big enough to be in control and to take care of His church. The question

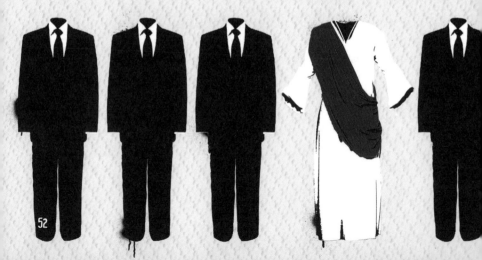

I had to spend time on was, "Is God in control? Is He taking care of His church?"

I wanted to say, "Yes, as long as we let Him." But if I can block Him from being in control of the church, I am bigger than He is.

As I wrestled with God on this, I wanted to say, "But God you don't know the church I know. You don't know the situation or the people I have to work with."

But what was driven home to me was the reality that not only is God in control, the real problem is He just doesn't consult with me as often as I think He ought to. In other words, the problem is my problem. I am really not trusting Him to be God.

As I have travelled around the world working with church members and leaders, I have seen a lot of the good of this church but I have also seen a lot of the problems and struggle we have in this church.

GOD IS IN CONTROL, THE REAL PROBLEM IS HE JUST DOESN'T CONSULT WITH ME AS OFTEN AS I THINK HE OUGHT TO.

Pastors and church leaders and members have opened their hearts about the struggles they face within and without—but they have also told me what God can do.

When I am tempted to think God may not be in control, He reaches out all around us and touches people. He is still a big God.

Presupposition 5: God provides everything we need

In His time frame, God provides everything we need to accomplish His will in His church.

Sometimes I am not willing to wait for God. Or sometimes my faith isn't big enough—I know what has to be done but I

COULD IT BE THAT I KNOW MY STAFF BETTER THAN I KNOW GOD?

just don't see the resources and I begin to say, "We've got to find the money, we have to raise it somehow."

When working on major projects, I have often had an assistant or secretarial staff and because of time constraints I have simply had to say, "You folks are going to handle all that." Then I work on my part of the project and trust they will do theirs.

But if I can trust my staff like that, why is it I struggle to trust God? Could it be that I know my staff better than I know God? Maybe our real struggle is not just to know the theory but to know Him well enough that we can integrate the theory in everyday life.

Presupposition 6: God works in partnership with us

God works in partnership with human agents.

Only rarely does God choose to work alone. He usually works in partnership, working through human agents.

Presupposition 7: Christ is Lord of all

Christ is Lord of all and lordship is a choice of our will.

His lordship is not something that is forced upon us. It is our choice whether Christ is going to be Lord.

Presupposition 8: The Holy Spirit is the active lordship agent

The Holy Spirit is the active lordship agent in our lives.

It is not about me working on you, you working on your child or neighbor, or us working on anybody else. It is God working in others.

What makes us think we can change anybody? But how often do we try to change each other in the church? Whose job is it to convict of sin and righteousness and judgment?

If it is the Holy Spirit's job to convict, then when I try to do that in your life or that of anybody else, including my own children, am I not usurping the role of the Holy Spirit?

And if He is not controlling the church and its leadership the way we think it ought to be, what makes us think that we can do so by withholding tithes or channeling tithes or money to other places?

In a sense, could this be seen as denying the Spirit of God? That sounds serious to me.

Presupposition 9: We receive the Holy Spirit by faith

Paul explained it like this: "Through the work of Christ Jesus, God has blessed the Gentiles with the same blessing he promised to Abraham, and we Christians receive the promised Holy Spirit through faith" (Galatians 3:14).

Jesus said, "If you sinful people know how to give good gifts to your children, how much more will your heavenly Father give the Holy Spirit to those who ask him" (Luke 11:13).

Ellen White wrote about how this works in *The Desires of Ages*. She reminds us that the power of the Holy Spirit is not ours if we seek to

"THE POWER OF GOD AWAITS THEIR DEMAND AND RECEPTION."

control Him instead of allowing Him to control us: "We cannot use the Holy Spirit. The Spirit is to use us" (page 672). But there is also the promise: "Only to those who wait humbly upon God, who watch for His guidance and grace, is the Spirit given. The power of God awaits their demand and reception" (page 672).

By faith, this blessing brings all other blessings. I never dreamed I had the right to demand anything of God but we are told this power claimed by faith, awaits our demand.

By faith, I can know I have the Holy Spirit.

Have you accepted it? It is that simple.

Presupposition 10: In Christ we are able to do anything He wants us to do

In Christ, we are able to do anything and everything He wants us to do.

Philippians 4:19 puts it like this: "And this same God who takes care of me will supply all your needs from his glorious riches, which have been given to us in Christ Jesus."

Which brings us to defining stewardship.

Stewardship is the lifestyle of one who accepts Christ's lordship, walking in partnership with God and acting as His agent to manage His affairs.

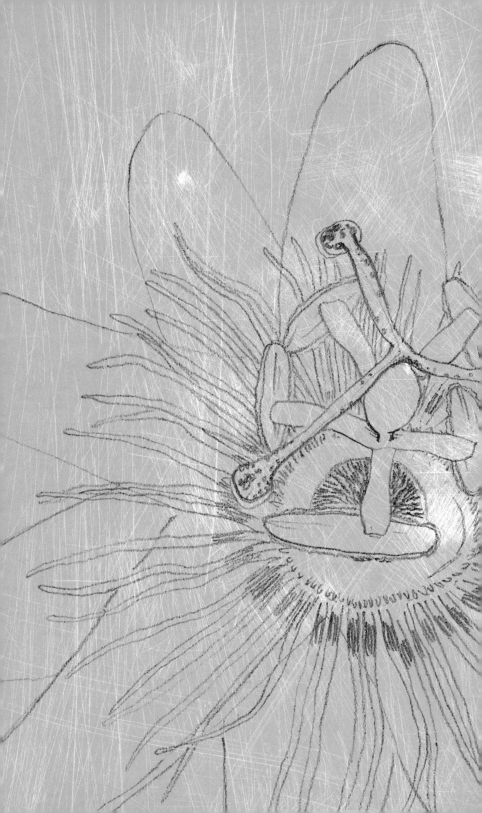

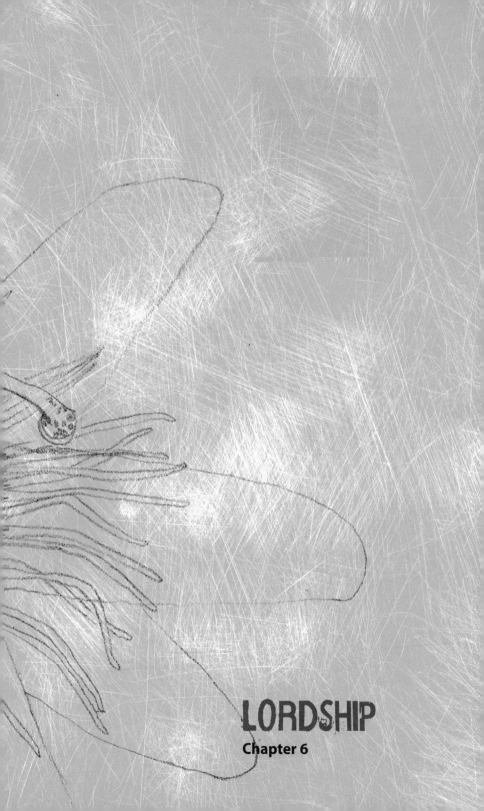

LORDSHIP

Chapter 6

This chapter is for the little Pharisee in each one of us. Often when we are talking about salvation and the Christian life in the way we have been, someone will ask, "But what about obedience?"

Obedience is important but it can come to be seen as a condition of our salvation. Obedience needs to be in the right place. The moment I think my obedience helps save me, I am in trouble. It becomes nothing more than legalism or salvation by works. Some of us have

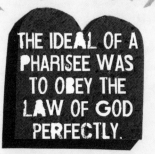

THE IDEAL OF A PHARISEE WAS TO OBEY THE LAW OF GOD PERFECTLY.

gotten to the point where we say, "We are saved by faith, but now we have got to work like the devil to stay saved." So we need to consider where obedience comes from and how it fits in the equation.

Don't be too hard on yourself if you find a little bit of Pharisee in yourself. The ideal of a Pharisee was to obey the law of God perfectly. The problem came when God walked in their midst and they didn't accept or recognize Him.

Model lordship

Perhaps we can use a model to help us understand the balance between a faith walk with God and obedience. This model describes different kinds of relationships with God using high and low ratings of performance (measured horizontally) and relationship (measured vertically).

Dabbler

Where both performance and relationship are low, we have people who could be described as dabblers. This is the person who only plays with their religion.

The picture I have of a dabbler is a person who goes out to the ocean,

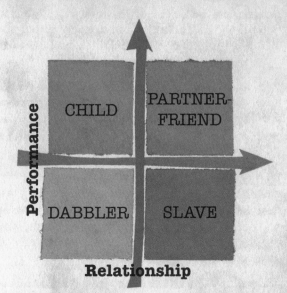

Performance (vertical axis), Relationship (horizontal axis)

CHILD	PARTNER-FRIEND
DABBLER	SLAVE

puts on their swimsuit but only splashes around with their toes in the water. They really don't enjoy the ocean. They are just kind of playing with it.

And we probably all know people who act like that with their faith. They don't take religion seriously.

Slave

But if we only emphasize performance—obedience, works—we produce a slave.

There are two sides to the legalism coin. The one we normally think of is a person who has a long list of things they have to do. They start checking them off, one after the other. And they put all kinds of things on the list. People even argue about what should be on the list. Legalism is simply a focus on our own performance.

The other kind of legalist is the person who says, "God doesn't require this long list of things for me. All God wants is these three things." But the focus remains on performance. We might think that person is a liberal because they don't have as much on their list. Yet they are just as legalistic because the focus is on what we do. And when we put the emphasis on performance, on obedience, on works, it produces a slave.

There are problems with performance by itself because, if we only have performance, the focus is on us. Not only that, it will make us judgmental because we begin to compare ourselves with others. But

RELIGION WITHOUT GOD IS NOTHING BUT ANOTHER FORM OF PAGANISM OR SLAVERY.

when we honestly look back at the mirror, we will always see our failures, faults and problems.

Performance is still what we are tempted to emphasize as a church. All our lifestyle issues, how to keep the Sabbath, our health message, Christian standards, all those things can draw us toward focusing on performance. And if focusing on performance without a relationship with Christ, it becomes a master–slave relationship. Religion without God is nothing but another form of paganism or slavery.

But we don't want to be in slavery. Slavery is the worst possible place to be. With all the right externals, it might look good but it is the subtlest form of paganism.

Jesus meets a performance slave

Remember the story of the rich young ruler who came to Jesus (see Matthew 19:16-22). He said to Jesus, "Teacher, what good things must I do to have eternal life?" (verse 16).

Jesus tells him to keep the commandments.

"I've obeyed all these commandments," the young man said proudly (verse 20).

Here is a man who has all the performance. Looking at him, everything was right. But what happens down deep?

Jesus tells him that he still lacks one thing: "If you want to be perfect, go and sell all you have and give the money to the poor, and you will have treasure in heaven. Then come, follow me" (verse 21). Jesus pointed him back to the relationship.

The story ends with the statement that "when the young man heard this, he went sadly away because he had many possessions" (verse 22). The Bible writer could have written that, "for many possessions had him."

This young man was a slave to his performance. He looks good; he has even been made a ruler in the Synagogue. That's why this is the worst place to be. We can look at ourselves and say, "What more do I need?"—until we recognize the emptiness in our hearts.

Have you ever been accused of being a legalist? Have you ever heard Seventh-day Adventists being accused of being legalist? Could it be because we are?

But when we tell people why we obey, what do we tell them? A common answer would be that we obey because we love God. Still many of us would say that we love God, yet how many of us obey completely?

This equation does not work in practice. We have said that if we love Him, we will obey, but love is not a motivation for obedience. Rather, love is a motivation for surrender and only the indwelling Christ can produce the obedience.

I am tired of a faith that focuses on doing and has little relationship. I am tired of a church that has a standard of behavior at one place and lives differently in another place. And the only difference I can tell is if God comes into our lives in a passionate love relationship.

Many people respond to these thoughts by saying that they are not comfortable with the use of the word *passion* when talking about our faith and walk with God. Passion deals with the basic things of life and it controls our emotions. It is what moves us and causes us to do things. But God says, "I have loved you, my people, with an everlasting love. With unfailing love I have drawn you to myself" (Jeremiah 31:3). God's passionate love is so great for us that it took Him to the cross.

I AM TIRED OF A FAITH THAT FOCUSES ON DOING AND HAS LITTLE RELATIONSHIP.

Any relationship without a passion grows stale and cold. But we cannot build a long-lasting relationship only on passion. There must be commitment and performance. But the issue is which fuels which. And they must work together.

There is only one cure for a slave. We call it death—and rebirth.

• On one occasion, Jesus said, "I assure you, unless you turn from your

sins and become as little children, you will never get into the Kingdom of Heaven" (Matthew 18:3).

• One night He talked with a Pharisee called Nicodemus and said, "Unless you are born again, you can never see the Kingdom of God" (John 3:3).

Jesus emphasized that what is needed is not simply to work harder or "better" but rather a new kind of life, a rebirth experience. If we begin with performance, we are only ever going to be slaves.

Child

If we put the emphasis only on relationship, it produces a child.

The problem with focusing only on relationship comes because this kind of relationship tends to look at the emotions, meaning how I feel today, and again that is a tendency to look at myself. Such an imbalance can also tempt us to be passive when it comes to performance, suggesting that obedience doesn't matter.

I think we would rather be a child than a slave because that means there is a relationship. But we don't want to be children forever.

If we have a two year old and all he can do is walk across the room that is OK. We don't expect that a two year old can walk across a busy street safely. But if he is about to turn 18 and he still can't walk across the

IT IS EASIER FOR A CHILD TO MATURE THAN A SLAVE TO BECOME PASSIONATE.

street, we would be concerned that this child has a problem. We want our children to grow—and if they don't, we will become concerned that they are not healthy.

A young child can communicate love to a parent or grandparent. He or she does it in simple ways—by a smile, a hug, a small gift or simply by saying so. But that child can do little for him or herself or for anyone else, no matter how much he or she loves them. They cannot care for or help anyone. They are high on the relationship scale but low on the performance scale. As we have said, that is OK when they are young but a healthy parental relationship will encourage them to grow up, mature and increase their performance abilities.

It is easier for a child to mature than for a slave to become passionate. While a child might not have high performance, the child has a deep relationship and is on a path that will draw them toward becoming a partner–friend. Because they already have a relationship, with disciplining, teaching and maturing, their relationship can grow into performance. That's why Jesus said becoming like little children (see Matthew 18:3) is a good place to be.

Partner–friend

In this model of lordship, the highest and deepest relationship to God is that of partner–friend. This is a relationship of high relationship and high performance. Like a slave, the partner–friend has high obedience but this obedience is in the context of the high relationship. The relationship is not based on the obedience.

"Partner–friend" is another way of describing the "normal Christian" stewardship relationship and experience we are exploring throughout this book.

A new birth—at 80

As a departmental church leader and a travelling speaker, I have had the privilege of leading more than 100 pastors to know Jesus Christ, many of them for the first time.

I will never forget a retired pastor who lived next door to the church where I met regularly with a small group of pastors. Every time we would meet there, he would argue with me as we explored what it meant to be a Christian and a pastor, what the biblical models of church and ministry are all about. He would always become uncomfortable when we talked about the relationship with God and he would struggle with what I was saying.

One day he was arguing with me and I had had enough. "In other words," I said, "what you do helped save you."

"What do you mean?" he said.

"You just said that your obedience helps earn part of your salvation," I continued.

"Well, isn't that right?" he replied.

"So it isn't a gift?"

And suddenly he realized what we had been saying. Then almost in his 80s, this man had been a missionary for more than 40 years and more years in pastoral ministry. And he began to weep as he realized that this whole time he had been teaching in a way that was producing slaves.

God had used him and his ministry to touch lives but he had realized that, in the way he was presenting it, obedience was part of the salvation equation. In his former understanding, what you did determined whether you were saved or lost, not whether or not you accepted the gift. And that day he wept tears that mixed sorrow and joy.

"Everybody needs to understand this," he said. "Everybody needs to see what I have just seen and that is that salvation can only be a gift.

"I have known in my head but I didn't realize I was teaching something else."

Through his tears, I believe that man became a partner–friend of God that day and his experience reminded me of the incredible gift God offers to us in such a relationship.

LOYALTIES
Chapter 7

Remember when you used to do tests at school. Were these for the benefit of the teacher or the student? A good teacher knows whether that student is a good student or poor student without any need for a test. But the teacher needs the test to justify the grade they are going to give that student.

But, more importantly, the student needs a test in order to know whether they have learned and understood the information.

In the same way, God has given us tests of our loyalty and relationship to Him. He knows where we are but He knows we need to be tested to know where we are in relation to Him.

The first test

The first test came in the Garden of Eden. Set in a perfect world, perfect human beings in a perfect relationship with God were tempted to become like gods (see Genesis 3:1-7).

But who were they already like? They already shared God's image and they shared intimacy, governance and dependence with God. The only thing they did not have was to be God themselves.

SET IN A PERFECT WORLD, PERFECT HUMAN BEINGS IN A PERFECT RELATIONSHIP WITH GOD WERE TEMPTED TO BECOME LIKE GODS.

Satan offers a counterfeit. He doesn't offer anything true and vibrant. The real question is that of ownership: Am I willing to let God be owner or am I going to be the owner? The questions behind this temptation are: Who really is God? To whom are we loyal? Who do we trust? Who do we obey? Who is lord of our lives?

Tests today

Today, God still wants us to test our relationship with and loyalty to Him. Two of those tests are the Sabbath in time and our use of tithe and possessions. But we must understand that these tests are for our benefit, not for God who knows us already or for others in the world around us. Remember, Jesus said the sign for the world that we are His disciples is how we love one another (see John 13:34, 35).

Recalling the sign of the covenant used most often in the Old Testament emphasizes the personal nature of these tests or signs. Circumcision was a sign for the believer himself. That was a way the believer acknowledged in his body that he accepted a covenant relationship with God. But it is not a sign you would go around showing off.

It is the same with the Sabbath and the tithe. Only two persons know if you are keeping the Sabbath. Only two persons know if you are tithing—you and God.

WE MUST UNDERSTAND THAT THESE TESTS ARE FOR OUR BENEFIT.

Because if you don't have the faith relationship with God and have not accepted Jesus as Savior, you can't keep the Sabbath and you can't tithe. It does not make any difference how much money you put in the offering envelope and mark it as tithe or how many days you keep holy.

The test is not the Sabbath or giving tithe. The real issue is, who is God? Behind every temptation, is a temptation to be our own gods and to be in control of our lives. Whether it's Sabbath or tithe, the issue is still loyalty to God. Am I willing to do it God's way and to trust Him?

You remember what Jesus said: "You have heard that the law of Moses says, 'Do not murder. If you commit murder, you are subject to judgment.' But I say, if you are angry with someone, you are subject to judgment! . . . You have heard that the law of Moses says, 'Do not commit adultery.' But I say, anyone who even looks at a woman with lust in his eye has already committed adultery with her in his heart" (Matthew 5:21, 22, 27, 28).

In His teaching, Jesus takes the rule and internalizes it into an attitude of where the heart is. That's why only the person who has a saving relationship with God can truly worship God in the Sabbath or in tithe and offerings.

Sabbath

Exploring Sabbath as a test of loyalty can help us understand some of the questions about tithe.

Sabbath is a question of putting God first and the Bible gives us a number of reasons for doing that:

1. Sabbath is a sign that I accept God as Creator.
In the Ten Commandments as recorded in Exodus 20, God's people were commanded to remember the Sabbath "for in six days the Lord made the heavens, the earth, the sea, and everything in them; then he rested on the seventh day. That is why the Lord blessed the Sabbath day and set it apart as holy" (Exodus 20:11).

2. Sabbath is a sign that I accept God as Redeemer.
When the Ten Commandments are repeated in Deuteronomy 5, the Fourth Commandment gives a different reason for remembering the Sabbath: "Remember that you were once slaves in Egypt and that the Lord your God brought you out with amazing power and mighty deeds.

That is why the Lord your God has commanded you to observe the Sabbath day" (Deuteronomy 5:15).

3. Sabbath is a sign that I accept God as Sanctifier.
There is another reason given for remembering the Sabbath in Exodus 31: "It helps you to remember that I am the Lord, who makes you holy" (Exodus 31:13). In other words, God says, remember I am your sanctifier, I can take care of your present life.

4. Sabbath is a sign that I accept God in my future.
Sabbath is also described as a sign and part of our eternal life in the New Earth: "All humanity will come to worship me from week to week and from month to month" (Isaiah 66:23). God says, on the Sabbath, remember I will care for your future.

Four principles for remembering Sabbath:
1. Accept the gift of salvation and eternal life. If we don't have that, we can't keep the Sabbath.
2. Seek intimacy with God.
3. Lay aside the burdens of life and the things of everyday life. Put God first in a specially focused way on the Sabbath.
4. Make it a day of worship and fellowship. Let the life focus around worshiping God and fellowshipping with Him and with other Christians.

In the gift of the Sabbath, God says to His people, "I am the God of the past, present and future. I take care of every part of your life." And Sabbath-remembering tests our acceptance of God's provision for us. The only person who can worship on the Sabbath is the person who has his or her faith placed in God: "So God's rest is there for people to enter. But those who formerly heard the Good News failed to enter because they disobeyed God" (Hebrews 4:6).

It is not just a matter of what I do or don't do on the Sabbath, it is about who has my heart.

Talking about money

Money was one of the themes mentioned most often by Jesus. Many of His parables deal with money or material possessions. Throughout the Bible, there are more than 2000 references dealing with money or material possessions, which is interesting to compare with only about 500 on prayer and less than 500 on faith. So many references suggest that God thought it an important topic for us to think about.

It is so important because money is life. Money does not buy life— but money is life. We can lose sight of this in today's world but it makes more sense if we recall the bartering system that is the beginning of our money systems.

MONEY DOES NOT BUY LIFE—BUT MONEY IS LIFE.

In a bartering system, people trade time, service, talent or product for someone else's time, service, talent or product. But the bartering system is awkward. If you had to exchange 50 bushels of wheat for a service, it was a big job to transport those 50 bushels. So people developed money as a medium of exchange. They started out with things like shells, rocks, precious stones or gold until they developed coins and finally paper money.

Issues of money are a spiritual battleground in the world, in the market place and in the home. Larry Burkett, a Christian financial counselor, reported that 80 percent of the divorcees in the United States list financial struggles as the primary contributing factor to a divorce.

Money is also a battleground in the church. The worst fights I have seen have been over how money is going to be spent. I remember one church board meeting where we went 45 minutes arguing about how to spend $25. That church board included a number of millionaires among its members. It wasn't an issue of $25; it was an issue of who was in control.

Money/God

God uses money. He uses it to advance His kingdom and to fund ministry. But money also competes with God in our lives.

In only a few places in the Bible is there a direct comparison between God and another god:

• Joshua made a call to following God at the time the Israelites were establishing themselves in the Promised Land: "But if you are unwilling to serve the Lord, then choose today whom you will serve. Would you prefer the gods your ancestors served beyond the Euphrates? Or will it be the gods of the Amorites in whose land you now live? But as for me and my family, we will serve the Lord" (Joshua 24:15).

• In his showdown with the priest of Baal on Mt. Carmel (see 1 Kings 18), Elijah put out a challenge: "How long are you going to waver between two opinions? If the Lord is God, follow him! But if Baal is God, then follow him!" (1 Kings 18:21).

• And Jesus used that same kind of contrast: "No one can serve two masters. For you will hate one and love the other, or be devoted to one and despise the other. You cannot serve both God and money" (Matthew 6:24).

Jesus makes such a direct comparison between God and money because money competes directly with God like other gods humans have devised. Money can be seen to represent life, power and assurance. It can give us a sense that we can take care of ourselves. We can even fool ourselves that if we have enough money, we don't really need God. And even the church is not immune to these temptations.

TIME AND MONEY MOST QUICKLY REFLECT OUR WALK WITH GOD AND IMPACT ON OUR WALK WITH GOD.

And because we use money as a means of exchange and sell our time to earn money, time and money are linked together in relation to God. If we change the way we deal with time, it will change the way we deal with God. If we change the way we deal with money, it will change the way we deal with God.

Time and money most quickly reflect our walk with God and impact on our walk with God. Maybe this is why God gave us the Sabbath and tithe as thermometers of our spiritual walk.

But, while money is an important part of stewardship, proper financial stewardship can only come in the context of the Christian lifestyle stewardship. We are not focusing just on money but we cannot ignore it because it reflects where we are in our walk with God.

Tithe with purpose

The usual purpose given for tithing is to support the ministry of the church. For example, the Bible story records one occasion when Abraham tithed to Melchizedek. This is the first time that tithe is mentioned in the Bible. The second time is when Jacob pledged to return a faithful tithe, but which church did Abraham and Jacob support with their tithe?

There was no church. There was no corporate "church" until Israel hundreds of years later.

And in Abraham's story, tithe is mentioned as if it is something normal and natural. Had he tithed at other times? Probably, but we have no record of what he did with the tithe. All we can assume is it was part of the worship service, perhaps burned up in offerings to worship God.

One of the purposes of tithe is to provide for full-time gospel ministry but this should not be seen as the primary motivation for tithing. Tithe as worship means I accept my relationship with God.

Worship by tithe

So the first and primary purpose of tithing is to worship God—to acknowledge Him as creator and owner, redeemer. When I worship God with my tithe, I accept God's ownership in everything that I am. I recognize God's care, His guidance and His love. I accept redemption as restoration of God's ownership. He is back in control.

Thankfulness is also part of the act of worship. And we understand that tithe is holy and belongs to the Holy One.

It is not about supporting the church. When we talk about tithe as designed to support the church, we rob people of the understanding of worshipping God. We don't tithe to the church; we tithe in worship to God.

WE DON'T TITHE TO THE CHURCH. WE TITHE IN WORSHIP TO GOD

When I think I am supporting the church, I am tempted to think it is my church and I have the right to manage it through my tithe. But it's God's church. I worship God by returning tithe to Him, acknowledging Him as owner and Creator. He then handles the tithes and supports the church. The tithe is His to administer, not mine.

That's not just words; it's a deep change of attitude and heart.

Combating selfishness

The second purpose for tithe is to combat selfishness by making God first. Tithe does not cure selfishness, the root of all sin for which the only cure is Jesus Christ. But for the person who walks with God, tithe becomes part of God's system for combating the selfishness in my old sinful nature and in the influences of the world around me.

As we have seen, tithe is the minimum test of loyalty in the material possessions. Do I acknowledge God as owner by giving back to Him what He says is His? Tithe reminds us of an unconditional surrender of everything we have.

Tithe is not a merit system. It is not a substitute for love, justice, mercy and loyalty. It is not a suggestion that the remainder is ours. But to not tithe denies God sovereignty, ownership, holiness and lordship. It denies His care and love.

TITHE REMINDS US OF AN UNCONDITIONAL SURRENDER OF EVERYTHING WE HAVE.

To not tithe denies His honor and glory, and it denies a divine partnership with Him.

Tithe is about who I am with God.

TITHING

Chapter 8

We have talked about the tests of loyalty—Sabbath, time, tithe, and financial and material possessions. But how are these tests?

It's like this. God says: "That is mine." Then we choose whether we are going to let Him have what is His. Are we going to claim ownership and say, "I have the right to do what I want to with *my* money"? That is something we say in different ways.

Do I recognize it as God's money, God's time, God's life, God's possessions? Or do I think I am the owner?

DO I RECOGNIZE IT AS GOD'S MONEY, GOD'S TIME, GOD'S LIFE, GOD'S POSSESSIONS?

So this is the test. In every issue of life—whether it's time, talent, treasure or our own minds—the bottom line is who we allow to be in control.

When it comes to the issue of tithe, a number of Bible passages challenge our choices when facing these tests. Let's explore the issue, the major conclusions of the Bible writers and the conclusions we can draw.

Abraham tithes

Read the story in Genesis 14.

The first mention of tithe in the Bible is the story of Abraham. God has already spoken to Abraham on several occasions. He has told Abraham that He will bless him and make him a blessing for all nations (see Genesis 12:1-3). And Abraham lives the balance of his life in response to these promises and blessings.

HE DOES NOT TITHE IN ORDER TO BE BLESSED. HE TITHES BECAUSE HE HAS BEEN BLESSED.

In fact, Abraham lives with a sense of God's presence in everything he does.

This is not something he arrives at overnight; it is a growth process.

We see Abraham developing and growing spiritually in his trust of God.

But we also see that Abraham is responding to these blessings. He does not tithe in order to be blessed. He tithes because he has been blessed.

At the beginning of the story in Genesis 14, Abraham receives the news that Sodom and Gomorrah have been attacked by a group of enemy kings. Sodom has been ransacked and the people of Sodom—including Abraham's nephew Lot and his family—have been taken captive.

Abraham gets together the 318 men of his household, which is obviously quite a large community. But even 318 men are not many to march against the combined forces of five kings. So the victory Abraham achieves is obviously something God has done. He has experienced God's blessing. He has been protected in battle and turns for home with the rescued prisoners and possessions of Sodom and Gomorrah.

On his way back from the battle, Abraham comes face to face with Melchizedek, the king of Salem. In response to God's blessing, his natural reaction is to give a tithe to God through Melchizedek.

You don't find God saying, "OK, Abraham, because I have blessed you now, you are to give me one-tenth." Nowhere in the earlier stories do we find a place where God tells Abraham what to do with tithes. We just see the first example as a normal practice. It seems it is something Abraham is used to doing already—a natural response to God's goodness to him and his family.

Jacob tithes

Read the story in Genesis 28.

The second mention of tithe in the Bible story is found in the story of Jacob.

Jacob has deceived his father. He had deceived his brother. He has tricked them into giving him the family birthright. When it is done, his mother says, "You better go. Go to my brother's house, because your brother will kill you the moment your father dies."

So Jacob is running away from home. He has been a deceiver and he is alone. Night comes and he lies down with only a rock for a pillow. But he is so tired he manages to sleep.

During the night, he is awakened by an incredible vision. He sees angels ascending and descending on a glorious ladder. God is at the top of the ladder. He says to Jacob, "I will be with you"—and He repeats the covenant of Abraham to Jacob, almost word for word.

IF YOU HAVEN'T RECEIVED ANY BLESSINGS, HOW CAN YOU TITHE?

As before, it is an unconditional covenant. God says, "I will do this because I am God. Not because of anything you do, but because of who I am. I will bless you and I will make you a blessing."

And then He adds to Jacob, "I will bring you back to your home—and I will be with you and bless you."

Jacob awakens. He says, "I have seen God." He calls the place Bethel, which means "the house of God." Jacob takes oil and pours it on the stone he has used as a pillow as an act of worship and then he says, "God, if you will be with me as you promised, if you bring me back and bless me with possessions, out of everything you give me, I will return to you a tenth."

Which comes first: the blessing or the tithe? The blessing. Throughout scripture we see the sequence: God blesses—and the response is worship through tithe. If you haven't received any blessings, how can you tithe? If you haven't been given anything, you don't have anything to tithe to God. This flow is repeated over and over again. Blessings from God: tithe as a response.

Jacob experiences God's presence. He hears God's promise. He commits to tithe as God continues to bless him.

Clear instructions

Those are the two first stories dealing with tithes. From here on, it is no longer the stories. Instead, there are clear instructions.

In Leviticus 27:30-33, the Israelites—the descendants of Abraham and Jacob—are told how to deal with tithe. Tithe belongs to God. Every tenth animal is "holy to the Lord." Interestingly, God shares in the risk with no selection by quality. In other words, even if the tenth animal is blind, lame or sick, it's still His animal. This contrasts with the instructions that animals given as offerings were to be perfect—without blemish. In tithing, God partners with His people, willing to share in the risks of this partnership.

In Numbers 18, God gives this tithe to the Levites. And this is the picture throughout the Old Testament. God gives blessing and the tithe is always returned to God as an act

IN TITHING, GOD PARTNERS WITH HIS PEOPLE, WILLING TO SHARE IN THE RISKS OF THIS PARTNERSHIP.

What about "offerings"?

"Offerings" suggest that we *offer* something to God. We tend to think of offering as sacrifice—and that is true—but we tend to think of sacrifice as something we give up, something we surrender, something that costs us.

But the only sacrifice God can accept from us is ourselves. Romans 12:1 urges, "And so, dear brothers and sisters, I plead with you to give your bodies to God. Let them be a living and holy sacrifice—the kind he will accept. When you think of what he has done for you, is this too much to ask?"

We are to offer all of ourselves to God. When we offer to God, He usually puts our offering back in our hands to administer for Him, in partnership with Him.

of worship to God, not to the Levites.

Then God gives the tithes to the Levites, but even the Levites were to tithe. No-one is exempt from tithing. It was part of the lifestyle of the Israelites.

Different tithe?

Verses in Deuteronomy Chapters 12, 14 and 26 suggest a different kind of tithe. It's the same word but the description is radically different. In Leviticus 27 and in Numbers 18, tithe is to be given to the Levites. But Deuteronomy suggests a "second tithe," uniquely different from the other tithe.

Of course, all tithe is about worshipping God. But the "second tithe" is about sharing God's blessings with those around us in a celebration feast together as a family and every third year it is given to the Levites and the poor. So it is different from the tithe of Leviticus and Numbers.

But there are other specific

THE AVERAGE ISRAELITE GAVE BETWEEN 25 AND 33 PERCENT OF THEIR INCOME BACK TO GOD ON A REGULAR BASIS.

instructions here about tithing, particularly about where the tithe is to be brought. God says, "Bring this tithe to the place the Lord your God chooses for his name to be honored" (Deuteronomy 14:23).

Comments in *Patriarchs and Prophets* and other historical sources tell us the average Israelite gave between 25 and 33 percent of their income back to God on a regular basis. The tenth specifically called a tithe as we use it today was used by the Levites for their support. The other tenth—and more—came in first fruits offerings, wave offerings and all the different kinds of offerings that they gave, as well as this other tithe talked about in Deuteronomy.

Revival = tithe

Many years later, Israel's King Hezekiah sparks a time of spiritual revival, recorded in 2 Chronicles 29 to 31. The temple is restored. The worship services are restored. The Passover is brought back and celebrated. People are called to return to God. In this context, the Levites are restored to their ministry and there is a call to return to tithing.

THIS IS THE FIRST TIME WE SEE A CALL TO REVIVAL ALONG WITH A CALL TO RETURN TO TITHING.

This is the first time we see a call to revival along with a call to return to tithing. Tithe is clearly presented in the context of God's blessings and 2 Chronicles 31:5-8 tells how the people responded.

Another time of revival is recorded in Nehemiah Chapters 10, 12 and 13. When Ezra reads the law, there is a commitment to faithfulness to God in tithes and offerings. In Nehemiah 13, we have storerooms built at the temple as a place to store the tithes and offerings brought in. This is the first time the term "storehouse" shows up in relation to tithing.

Tithing tests?

In Amos 4, God is mocking His people. He says, "Go on with your different kinds of sin. And go on with your tithes and offerings. See if they do you any good." In other words, He is challenging their tithes in the context of their life of sin. Can you separate tithe from your heart relationship? No. God is really saying that tithe is an external act reflecting where the heart is.

BUT WHAT DO WE SAY TO THE OLD LADY OR THE FAMILY WHO REMAIN POOR ALL THEIR LIVES, DESPITE BEING FAITHFUL WITH TITHE? DID GOD LIE?

But Malachi 3:8-12 is probably the worst used, most often misquoted passage on tithes and offerings: "'You have cheated me of the tithes and offerings due to me. You are under a curse, for your whole nation has been cheating me. Bring all the tithes into the storehouse so there will be enough food in my Temple. If you do,' says the Lord Almighty, 'I will open the windows of heaven for you. I will pour out a blessing so great you won't have enough room to take it in! Try it! Let me prove it to you! Your crops will be abundant, for I will guard them from insects and disease. Your grapes will not shrivel before they are ripe,' says the Lord Almighty. 'Then all nations will call you blessed, for your land will be such a delight,' says the Lord Almighty."

How often have we presented stewardship as business bargain with God? If we are faithful with our tithes and offerings, we say or think, God has to bless us and make us rich.

But what do we say to the old lady or the family who remain poor all their lives, despite being faithful with tithe? Did God lie? No, the preacher just did not understand scripture. Because that is not what the promise is about.

Malachi 3 comes in the context of an extended dialogue about apostasy. It begins with Chapter 1. God says, "This is what you have done."

And the people argued with Him: "What do you mean we have done that?"

So God explains to them how they have gone wrong. And this dialogue continues, back and forth, between God and His people.

Finally, in Chapter 3, God says, "Come back to me."

"How should we come back to you?" the people ask.

"In the areas where you have robbed Me," says God.

"How have we robbed you?"

"In tithes and offerings," God replies.

God is saying, "I have been blessing you and you have been robbing Me. Now test Me and see if faithfulness to Me is not better than unfaithfulness."

He is not saying, "If you are a tither, I will bless you." Rather God is saying, "I have blessed you and you have robbed Me. Now return what is Mine, what belongs to Me."

Clearly, there is a promise of God's blessings tied with it. But the tithe is never a condition of God's blessings. It is always a response to God's blessings, even here in Malachi.

Again, there is a call to return to God, this time one of the ways to do this is to acknowledge their "robbery," where there has been a failure to recognize God's past blessings.

New Testament tithing

Jesus' teaching about tithing both affirms the responsibility and puts it in a right perspective. Matthew 23, Luke 11 and 18 are basically parallel passages where tithe is presented as an expected response to God, in explaining how the religious practices of the Pharisees fell short.

Jesus says, "How terrible it will be for you teachers of religious law and you Pharisees. Hypocrites! For you are careful to tithe even the tiniest part of your income, but you ignore the important things of the law—justice, mercy, and faith. You should tithe, yes, but you should not leave undone the more important things" (Matthew 23:23).

Jesus is saying that tithe is important but must be recognized in context of a worship lifestyle of justice and mercy. If you don't have the right heart relationship with God, your tithe is not acceptable.

The final mention of tithing in the Bible is found in Hebrews 7. Again, tithing is presented as a command and the Levites are presented as having been commanded to receive the tithe.

This passage reviews the story of Abraham and Melchizedek. Jesus is presented as a priest "in the line of Melchizedek" (Hebrew 7:17). He is a greater priest than Aaron or the Levites because they were priests in a merely human linage and their ancestor Abraham had tithed to this higher line of priesthood.

But the point in relation to tithing: it is still presented as a command, as something expected in a relationship with God.

JESUS IS SAYING THAT TITHE IS IMPORTANT BUT MUST BE RECOGNIZED IN CONTEXT OF A WORSHIP LIFESTYLE OF JUSTICE AND MERCY.

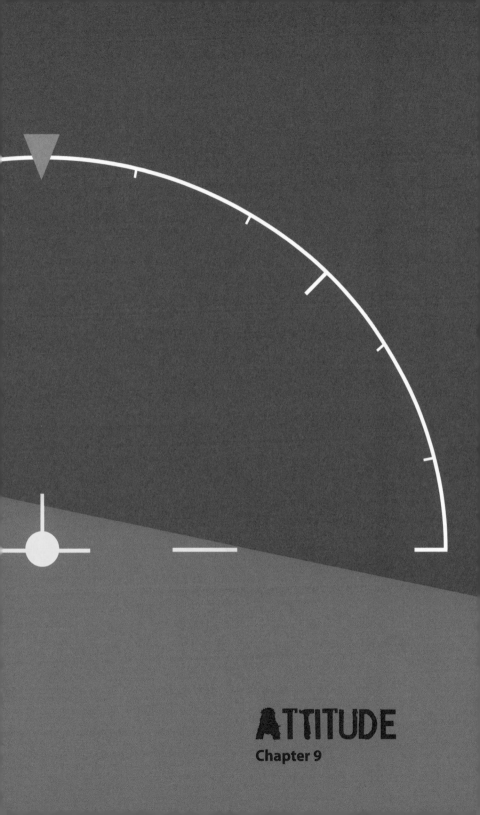

ATTITUDE

Chapter 9

Rock Hamilton

1732

Loyalty determines who we serve. Attitude determines how we serve. And we need to consider both.

It is not enough just to say I am going to serve God because He says I have to. It needs to be a response out of a positive, loving attitude that knows and walks with God. A test of attitude is just as true as a test of loyalty.

Jesus said, "You must love the Lord your God with all your heart, all your soul, and all your mind" (Matthew 22:37). He said, "Take my yoke upon **A TEST OF ATTITUDE IS JUST AS TRUE AS A TEST OF LOYALTY.** you. Let me teach you, because I am humble and gentle, and you will find rest for your souls. For my yoke fits perfectly, and the burden I give you is light" (Matthew 11:29, 30). Jesus was talking about a new attitude to living.

Questions of attitude

Attitude is about how we serve God and whether we serve Him fully. The setting is daily life. It is what we do with God—not on Sabbath, not with the 10 percent, but the other six days of the week and with the other 90 percent—with everything that we are. Where are our mind and our heart? Where do we invest our time? Where is our treasure?

To examine our attitudes, consider the following questions:

1. Who do we live for?

Paul's answer to this was "For to me, living is for Christ" (Philippians 1:21).

The Romans had a problem with Paul: What do you do with a man who is already dead? All you can do is bury him.

PAUL'S WHOLE LIFE WAS WRAPPED UP IN WHO HE LIVED FOR IN JESUS CHRIST.

95

They tried to threaten Paul, saying, "If you don't quit preaching, we are going to send you to Rome in chains."

To which Paul would respond, "I would do anything to go to Rome and preach the gospel there."

Then they would say, "Paul, if you don't quit preaching, we are going to beat you."

And he says, "I rejoice in the sufferings of my Lord."

Again they threaten Paul, "If you don't quit preaching, we are going to put you to death."

Paul says, "For me to die is gain."

"OK, Paul, if you don't quit preaching, we are going to keep you alive but in prison."

Paul just smiles and says, "For to me, living is for Christ."

So what could they do? Paul's whole life was wrapped up in Who he lived for in Jesus Christ.

2. Who do we live with?

And Paul's attitude is also *with* Christ: "I have been crucified with Christ. I myself no longer live, but Christ lives in me. So I live my life in this earthly body by trusting in the Son of God, who loved me and gave himself for me" (Galatians 2:19, 20).

This is the attitude portrayed in Ezekiel 36:26, 27: "I will give you a new heart with new and right desires, and I will put a new spirit in you. I will take out your stony heart of sin and give you a new, obedient heart. And I will put my Spirit in you so you will obey my laws and do whatever I command" (see also Philippians 2:13).

It is the same idea through it all: Do I live in such a relationship with God that I live *with* Him?

3. How do we live?

Romans 6 is written for narrow-minded people. Paul begins by asking, "Should we keep on sinning so that God can show us more and more kindness and forgiveness? Of course not!" (verses 1, 2).

Why not? Because if you have been baptized in Christ, you have been baptized into His death and raised into His life. We all die the second death but the choice is when and where. Do we die on our own at the end of the millennium or do we die in Christ at Calvary?

WE ALL DIE BUT THE CHOICE IS WHEN AND WHERE.

When you accept Christ, you have died with Christ and been raised into His eternal life. That is why Paul writes in verse 11, "So you should consider yourselves dead to sin and able to live for the glory of God through Christ Jesus."

In verse 14, Paul exults in the new power that is now controlling our lives: "Sin is no longer your master, for you are no longer subject to the law, which enslaves you to sin. Instead, you are free by God's grace."

Today's attitude tests

There are two important tests of our attitude to God in our lives today:

Time

There is a two-fold intimacy in time. Do we take time with God daily in devotional time and do we integrate Him into every area of life? In any relationship, the level of our passion—our attitude to the other person—is in direct proportion with the level of intimacy. If you want more passion, build intimacy—which comes from time spent together.

Possessions

God also has a contemporary test in relation to our material stuff. Tithe comes first—God says, "That is Mine." That is a test of our loyalty and as we have seen God expects one-tenth of our income as tithe.

Then come offerings, regular systematic support given as offerings as part of worshipping to God.

Then comes giving to special projects.

The integrated life

When our relationship with God is integrated into our life, we apply

HOW DOES MY PASSION CONTROL MY USE OF TIME AND POSSESSIONS?

the love and passion everyday by answering the question who or what is the practical passion of my life. For example, how does my love for God change my relationship with others?

We are testing our attitude. Because of what being a Christian means, we walk with and live with God, making Christ a priority in all our decisions. How does my passion control my use of time and possessions? Is it focused on me or is it focused on God?

We are coming back to the same issues that we discussed earlier when describing disciples. It's about accepting Him as Lord and accepting the Holy Spirit as the active agent and seeking His will first before acting, before making a decision.

Somebody asked me once when we were studying this subject, "Does that mean that if you accept Christ, you can do anything you want to?"

"Absolutely not!" was my reply.

God has clear boundaries. He said, "These things I want you to do; these things I don't want you to do." We discover those boundaries in God's Word. And these are part of living in God and having the right attitude in doing that. Usually an attitude problem will reveal itself when we begin testing or resisting God's boundaries.

Giving better

Before we can have the grace of giving, we must have the grace of receiving. Jesus told His disciples to "Give as freely as you have received!" (Matthew 10:8). And "God so loved the world that He *gave . . .*" We accept Christ, then we have something to give.

The grace of giving is preceded by making God first. This includes giving of one's self, offering ourselves as a living sacrifice (Romans 12:1). You can't buy God off. You can't give Him money, if He doesn't have your heart.

WHEN GIVING OFFERINGS, WE ARE TEMPTED TO THINK THAT GOD DOESN'T HAVE ENOUGH MONEY, SO HE IS GOING TO USE SOME OF OURS.

As an antidote for selfishness, offerings become an expression of gratitude. Tithe is a recognition of who He is; offerings are an expression of gratitude. Offerings are an agent of transforming grace. As we give, we participate in God's grace, thus combating selfishness. It is a response to God's giving, implementing the partnership of God and working from God's abundance, rather than humanity scarcity.

When giving offerings, we are tempted to think that God doesn't have enough money, so He is going to use some of ours. But when we look at Bible examples, we soon recognize that these gifts were not about God's need but were concerned with the attitude of the giver:

• When God asked Abraham to offer his son, He was not needing or wanting a human sacrifice; instead He was testing Abraham's priorities and faithfulness (see Genesis 22).

• When Elijah asked the widow of Zarephath to bake a cake

for him first, she was blessed with enough food for her and her son to continue to eat—and when her son did die, he was resurrected (see 1 Kings 17).

• Jesus recognized the attitude of the woman who gave just "two pennies" at the temple as more valuable than the large offerings others were giving (see Mark 12:41-44).

• Paul praised the Macedonian believers for their generosity amid poverty: "Though they have been going through much trouble and hard times, their wonderful joy and deep poverty have overflowed in rich generosity" (2 Corinthians 8:2).

When we consider offerings, the motive is always more important than the amount. God operates on maximums, not minimums. We should give as the Holy Spirit convicts and give with no strings attached, without control. If we are still trying to control it, we have never really given it—all we are doing is managing our investment somewhere else.

How much should I give?

When it comes to giving offering, there are just two principles:

• As God has blessed you; and
• As He convicts you in your own heart.

I can't say you ought to give a second tithe or third tithe because, if I tell you the minimum you ought to give in the offering is a second tithe and all God expects you to give is 3 percent, you are going to feel guilty. But if I tell you, you have to give you a second tithe and God is trying to tell you, you ought to give 30 or 40 percent, you are going to feel satisfied and I am going to rob either one of you of that worship experience with God.

Neither should the church tell us how much to give. If it does, it is trying to do God's work.

Only the Holy Spirit can move somebody's heart to that point. Offerings are a test of my attitude and it is not about how much I give but who guides my giving.

God's purpose for offerings

1. To extend the partnership of humanity.
2. To give a testimony of praise to God.
3. To support His mission on earth.
4. To strengthen the unity of the church.
5. To provide for His church in order to help the needy.

The Holy Spirit's role in giving:

1. To convict and guide the giver.
2. To empower or make it possible for the giver to give.
3. To guide the corporate body and its leadership in using what is given.

Sharing Him

Another aspect of this intimacy is actively sharing Christ with those around us, particularly by telling our own story of what God is currently doing in our life. It is wonderful to tell how Jesus transformed us when we accepted Him. But a testimony that might be decades old is not as meaningful as a story of the God I walked with and who touched my life yesterday.

Sharing our stories of God's actions in our lives and making disciples are an extension of life lived with God. I help make disciples by telling my stories and helping people know how to walk with Jesus. That's my ministry. When we do this, we have the joy of seeing people grow with God.

The gospel commission is "As you go, make disciples" (see Matthew 28:19, 20). This is a privilege all of us can have as Christians. And if you think what you do is not focused on this, perhaps you need to check your attitude. What does a mother do with the children? What does a teacher do? What does a deacon do? As ministers of Christ, whatever we do is about making disciples.

I HELP MAKE DISCIPLES BY TELLING MY STORIES AND HELPING PEOPLE KNOW HOW TO WALK WITH JESUS.

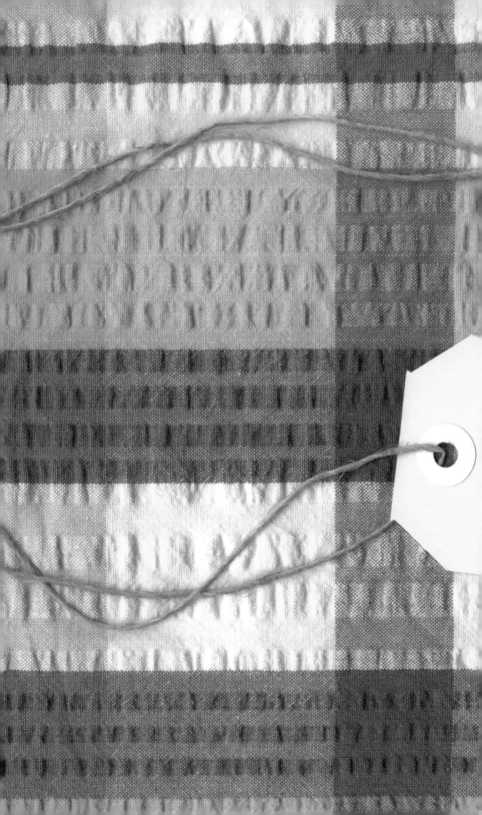

PARTNERS

Chapter 10

YOURS

Let's return to our definition of stewardship: "Stewardship is the lifestyle of the one who accepts Christ's lordship and walks in partnership with God, acting as His agent in managing His affairs on earth."

Every part of our lives belongs to God. We walk with Him—and we manage His assets and His business on this earth. One of the key things this means is that we have to learn to transfer ownership. There are some real problems with ownership. If we think we are owners, it leads to a confused identity and gives us a false sense of responsibility, tempting us to worry beyond our level of responsibility.

EVERY PART OF OUR LIVES BELONGS TO GOD.

Jesus said, "So don't worry about having enough food or drink or clothing. Why be like the pagans who are so deeply concerned about these things? Your heavenly Father already knows all your needs, and he will give you all you need from day to day if you live for him and make the Kingdom of God your primary concern" (Matthew 6:31-33).

Reality check

It is important for us to face the reality of ourselves:

• We give lip service to God as owner but few of us really accept God as owner. Most of us in our Christian life would like to think that God is owner but, in our everyday activities, it is not so simple. Too often we would rather try to live the Christian life in our own strength than die to ourselves.

IF WE DID REALLY GIVE CONTROL TO HIM, SOME OF THE THINGS WE DO AND TRY TO FORCE EACH OTHER TO DO WOULD CHANGE.

- Few of us have learned to release control of all to Him. This applies to our everyday lives, the big decisions and events in our lives, and to God's control of the church. If we did really give control to Him, some of the things we do and try to force each other to do would change.
- We have an ingrained premise that ownership means security and independence, success, happiness, status and absence of worries. In reality, ownership means just the opposite.

"Ownership" problems

Ownership produces responsibility but if you are not the owner, is it a false responsibility? And it is a responsibility that you can never fulfill.

We are afraid that we will never have enough, that somebody is going to take it away from us and we always want more. This constant fear adds to our worry and sense of frustration.

A sense of ownership also leads us to think we are in control. And when we don't feel in control when we think we are supposed to be, it leads us to try harder and push harder, starting a vicious cycle. We have to break this cycle and let God be in control.

WE BECOME THE OWNED INSTEAD OF THE OWNER.

If we want to control something, it eventually ends up trying to control us. So one of the real problems with claiming ownership and trying to control things is we end up submitting the control of our lives to that thing. We become the owned instead of the owner.

We are really not even responsible for our next breath. We think we are going to get up tomorrow but tomorrow we might not even be here. Ultimately, we are not in control and never can be.

And, of course, we cannot take possessions with us. They don't belong

YOURS

to us anyway. Somebody asked the lawyer of a great wealthy man when he died, how much he left behind when he died. The lawyer simply answered, "Everything." We can't take it with us.

As Jesus said, "Why be like the pagans who are so deeply concerned about these things?" This is the reality. This is a pagan lifestyle.

Letting God be owner requires a total surrender of our self to Him.

Prioritizing God's way

There are a number of practical ways in which we can prioritize God's way:

Put Him first.

As Jesus put it, "Live for him and make the Kingdom of God your primary concern" (Matthew 6:33).

Transfer.

Peter wrote, "Give all your worries and cares to God, for he cares about what happens to you" (1 Peter 5:7).

Some of us need to look around our lives and transfer all parts of our lives back to Him. We need to put our hands on the doorpost of our house and say, "God I transfer ownership of this house to You. This is Your house. I thought it was mine but I now give it back to You."

Perhaps we need to put our hands on the steering wheel of the car we drive and say, "God this is Your car. I have claimed it as mine but it's Yours." Look at the other stuff we have in our homes and ask ourselves whether we need to give them back to the God who really owns it all.

SOME OF US NEED TO LOOK AROUND OUR LIVES AND TRANSFER ALL PARTS OF OUR LIVES BACK TO HIM.

The same applies to our families, whether parents, children, spouse, brothers or sisters. We need to say, "God,

I give this person to You. I love them and recognize that You've put them in my hands to care for on Your behalf but I know they are Yours." Imagine how this might change our relationships. We are tempted to think it is our job to change people and exercise control over them. But we need to surrender our loved ones to God and see what happens in their lives and our relationships.

We need to transfer ownership of everything. We only hold these things in trust. They don't belong to us.

Treasure.

Jesus said, "Wherever your treasure is, there your heart and thoughts will also be" (Matthew 6:21).

Put your heart where your treasure is and put your treasure where your heart is, which for someone seeking to follow God means placing your treasure with God. This does not necessarily mean giving everything you have in offering. But make sure He has all the treasure anyway so He can do with it what He wants to. It is not yours. It belongs to Him. So follow His guidance. You manage—He guides.

Let God supply.

"And this same God who takes care of me will supply all your needs

from his glorious riches, which have been given to us in Christ Jesus"
(Philippians 4:19).

God's divine power has given us everything we need for life—so let
God supply all your needs. There is nothing you face that He can't
change for you.

A significant aspect of this is how we relate to money. As we have
seen, God's greatest competitor is money. It can give us a sense of
confidence and power. But no-one can serve two masters, so let's
compare God's way or the way of money offered us by Satan:

God's way	Satan's way
Love Jesus	Love money
Provide all our needs	Death
Freedom to depend on Him	Slavery
Trusteeship	Ownership
Partnership with God	Rob God
Giving is better	Bigger is better
Contentment	More is success
Trust	Distrust
Restore His image in us	Despise
Give to help others	Hoard
Joy	Grief
Now and eternity	Now only
Peace	Anxiety

Satan has a golden chain with which he binds us: "People who long
to be rich fall into temptation and are trapped by many foolish and
harmful desires that plunge them into ruin and destruction. For the
love of money is at the root of all kinds of evil. And some people,
craving money, have wandered from the faith and pierced themselves
with many sorrows" (1 Timothy 6:9, 10).

But contrast that with the way God looks at things: "Stay away from
the love of money; be satisfied with what you have. For God has said,
'I will never fail you. I will never forsake you.'

That is why we can say with confidence, 'The Lord is my helper, so I will not be afraid. What can mere mortals do to me?'" (Hebrews 13:5, 6).

It is two different lifestyles. Either we are tied with God's golden chains of love and a full reliance on Him where He provides all we need, everything we need for life and godliness, or we are bound by the devil to the chains of greed and selfishness, looking for power and control, status and standing in our own strength.

Partnership

God is seeking that we live in partnership with Him, meaning shared relationship. This was a principle of the story of Creation. This includes intimate sharing in a number of important ways:

1. Shared image and governance. In God's plan, God's image and governance are restored in His people as they were originally created in human beings.

2. Shared respect. God respects our freedom of choice. He does not force us. In turn, we respect His power and who He is.

3. Shared values. As we open our lives to Him, God's values for life become ours.

4. Shared tasks. We become participants and partners with Him in the mission of redemption, reconciling the world to God.

5. Shared goals. We let God's goals become our goals and define success differently than when the world is in control.

6. Shared resources. Everything we have belongs to Him. But that is not the half of it. Everything He has is available to us as resources for everyday living and for working with Him. We can easily

EVERYTHING HE HAS IS AVAILABLE TO US AS RESOURCES FOR EVERYDAY LIVING AND FOR WORKING WITH HIM.

forget about the huge amount in God's bank account and operate just from our poverty instead of His wealth and riches.

7. Shared risks. Partnership means God shares the risk with us. Look at how much God risked in giving His Son. Compared with that, is there any risk on our part when we invest with Him? He is really the One who takes all the risks.

8. Shared rewards. Describing us as co-heirs of God, the Bible says, "Everything God gives to his Son, Christ, is ours, too" (Romans 8:17). Imagine living the rest of eternity as God's representatives from and on His throne. I am not quite sure what that means but I can't wait to find out.

Different prosperity

When we have this kind of partnership relationship with God, we begin to measure prosperity differently from how it is often judged by the world around us.

Prosperity can be a blessing or a curse, depending on how we react to it. For example, if being a millionaire would make it more difficult for you to walk with God, would you really want to be a millionaire? But real prosperity is making sure there is enough—and God does that.

We sometimes give the idea that if somebody has a lot of money,

WE NEED TO DEFINE HOW MUCH IS ENOUGH THE WAY GOD DOES.

they have been blessed and God is good to them because they were good. But at other times, we say, if someone has a lot of money, it must be because they were crooked in some way. And if they are poor, they are holy. But prosperity is not a sign of spirituality. Neither is the opposite—poverty—a sign of spirituality.

There is a danger in trusting in money instead of God. But we need to understand the difference between hoarding and saving. Saving and being careful with money is an attitude of prudent planning but it should not be about trying to build power or security based on money in the bank. There is wisdom in saving so we don't have to go in debt and to take care of an emergency. But that is different from hoarding. A lot of people save because they are afraid to trust in God. They want to have enough to take care of themselves and hoarding is an attitude that there is never enough.

The purposes of prosperity and resources are to provide for the needs and comfort of the family, help the needy and help finance God's kingdom. Any other reason is hoarding. In considering this, we need to recognize the difference between needs, wants and desires.

But how much is enough? That's something I can't answer for you. There are two—or three, if you are married—people who will know: you, your spouse and God. Some of us need to open up our bank accounts to God and let Him have full control, but that does not necessarily mean emptying our bank accounts and giving all our money to the church. As we have been saying, this is about letting God have such control that He can do what He wants, when He wants to.

True contentment or peace comes from God. We need to define how much is enough the way God does. Let God transform your needs, wants and desires.

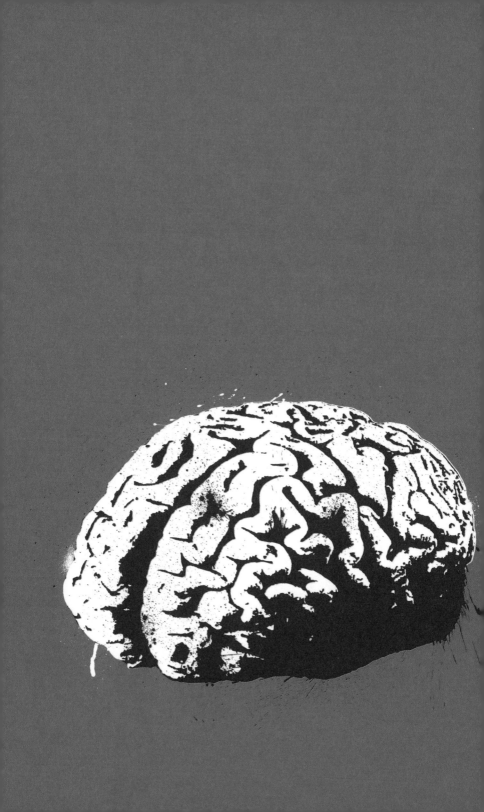

TRANSFORMATION
Chapter 11

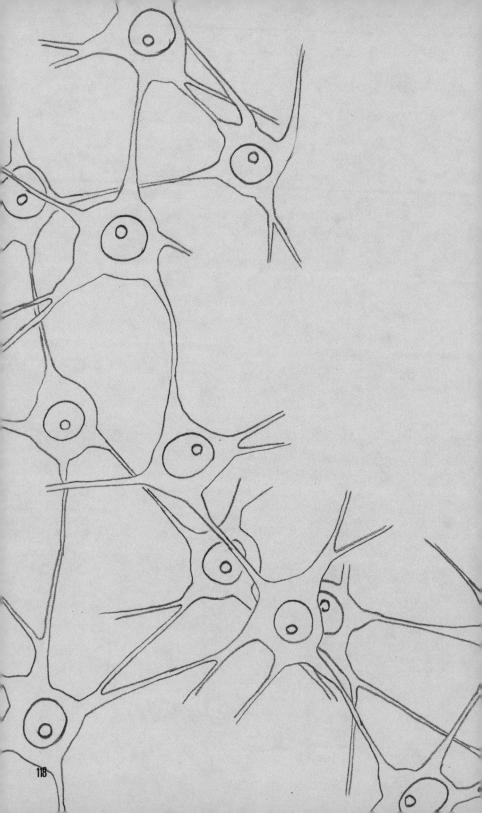

In our exploration of discipleship, we have talked about transferring ownership and making decisions about Who is in control. But the most incredible asset God has given us is the human mind. Paul explained it like this: "Don't copy the behavior and customs of this world, but let God transform you into a new person by changing the way you think. Then you will know what God wants you to do, and you will know how good and pleasing and perfect his will really is" (Romans 12:2).

Your mind

There is a lot of new research on the mind today—medically and psychologically. The mind is an incredible gift and it has incredible potential.

The mind is God's ultimate gift in the creation of human beings. In the human brain, all of our life is controlled. Much of even the physical side of things is determined by the mind, with many diseases linked to people's state of mind.

The mind is also where the habits are formed, which are physical pathways laid down in the brain. And the mind is where the relationship with God takes place, as well as where the battle with sin is fought.

THE MIND IS WHERE THE RELATIONSHIP WITH GOD TAKES PLACE, AS WELL AS WHERE THE BATTLE WITH SIN IS FOUGHT.

The human brain is incredibly complex. On average, we have between 80 and 100 billion brain cells. Each of those brain cells can have up to 1000 interconnections with other cells and has the information storage capacity equal to 30 times the entire *Encyclopedia Britannica*. Then add in the processing and judgment capacity, and the brain's capacity to grow and develop. Within each brain cell, they have discovered traces of every hormone and every chemical substance found in the body.

As I mentioned, thoughts and actions are electrical chemical messages and their pathways are physical structures that are created in our brains. If we repeat the same reaction to the same stimulus over and over again, it begins to build a habit, with reactions to certain situations becoming easier and more direct.

The good news is this process has incredible potential but, negatively, once a habit is built, it can never be completely done away with. At best, we will always have a tendency or temptation to respond according to our established habits when we receive sufficient stimulus.

Changing your mind

Because our old natures want to go down the old pathways, we have to immerse our minds in Christ, focusing on Him everyday. This sets our lives in the context of Jesus and His sacrifice. And over time this changes our old pathways and builds new habits in our minds.

That's why it is so important that we resist the devil because we need to say a defini   ho. It puts the brakes on the old pathway and, submitting to G , it opens a new pathway. But if we play with temptation in our minds, our mind will eventually be triggered toward the old pathway.

Of course, this is a physical, scientific explanation of how God works in the human mind, transforming the mind on a structural level. But let's also consider some Bible references about the mind:

• Quoting Deuteronomy 6:4, 5, Jesus said, "You must love the Lord your God with all your heart, all your soul, all your mind, and all your strength" (Mark 12:30).

• As well as urging that our minds be transformed (see Romans 12:2), Paul urged that "all of us have had that veil removed so that we can be mirrors that brightly reflect the glory of the Lord. And as the Spirit of the Lord works within us, we become more and more like him and reflect his glory even more" (2 Corinthians 3:18).

• He also assured us we can understand the things of God, with the help of the Holy Spirit, "for we have the mind of Christ" (1 Corinthians 2:16).

• In Philippians 2:5-8, Paul expanded on what it means to have the mind of Christ: "Your attitude should be the same that Christ Jesus had. Though he was God, he did not demand and cling to his rights as God. He made himself nothing; he took the humble position of a slave and appeared in human form. And in human form he obediently humbled himself even further by dying a criminal's death on a cross."

• "Don't worry about anything; instead, pray about everything. Tell God what you need, and thank him for all he has done. If you do this, you will experience God's peace, which is far more wonderful than the human mind can understand. His peace will guard your hearts and minds as you live in Christ Jesus" (Philippians 4:6, 7).

The Bible is clear that we should focus our minds on true and heavenly things.

Make the change

So let me recommend some practical steps toward making a change in our thinking and allowing God to transform our minds:

1. Prayerfully face your sinful reality.

OVER TIME THIS CHANGES OUR OLD PATHWAYS AND BUILDS NEW HABITS IN OUR MINDS.

We are sinners. Without Christ, we have no hope. And every morning we have to face this reality. Throughout his letters, Paul did it regularly. Even though there is nothing negative recorded about the prophet Daniel in the Bible story, when he prayed to God about a problem he was facing and he didn't understand the prophecy, he began by confessing his sin before God (see Daniel 9).

2. Gratefully accept your reality in Christ Jesus.

Don't just accept how you feel as a sinner but accept what God says about who you are in Him. If you have accepted Him as your Savior, you can know you are forgiven. You are cleansed and clothed in His righteousness. You are holy. You are a saint. You are sitting on the throne and living from the throne. It is a choice of the will to accept His Word, not because of anything we have earned or done but simply because He promised it.

3. Focus your mind on Christ and things above.

Hebrews 12:1, 2 explains it like this: "Let us strip off every weight that slows us down, especially the sin that so easily hinders our progress. And let us run with endurance the race that God has set before us. We do this by keeping our eyes on Jesus, on whom our faith depends from start to finish. He was willing to die a shameful death on the cross because of the joy he knew would be his afterward." And what is the joy Jesus was pursuing? It is us—we are His joy (see Zephaniah 3:17). So set your mind on things above and remember this perspective on who you are.

Paul described this attitude similarly: "Since you have been raised to new life with Christ, set your sights on the realities of heaven, where Christ sits at God's right

SET YOUR MIND ON THINGS ABOVE AND REMEMBER THIS PERSPECTIVE ON WHO YOU ARE.

hand in the place of honor and power. Let heaven fill your thoughts" (Colossians 3:1, 2). We are to live our lives with an awareness of Him and in tune with Him.

4. Be willing to live with the mystery of God.

When we come to a relationship with God, we need to accept that there are some things about God we cannot understand and some questions we cannot answer. You have to just accept some things based on the fact that God says it. God is so much bigger than we are.

5. Practice the presence of God.

Practicing God's presence is opening our mind to the reality of God, accepting His promise to be with us always (see Matthew 28:20). It is accepting the Holy Spirit by faith. It is opening the imagination to the reality of God and making room for Him in our life.

6. Actively resist sin.

We need to make a choice. James said, we should "resist the devil, and he will flee from you" (James 4:7). So make a solid, firm decision and resist him.

RESIST THE DEVIL AND HE WILL FLEE FROM YOU.

7. Practice devotional skills.

We will explore this below.

Practicing devotional skills

Spiritual disciplines are the tools of discipleship and the devotional skills are what we want to focus on.

Regular planned time for devotional life.

We need to have a regular planned time for the devotional life. If we don't, it isn't going to happen. We will be so busy dealing with the urgent, we will never get to doing the important.

We don't want to go to the other extreme of thinking we earn salvation through a devotional life. I have been there. I used to have my devotional life so well planned out that for three months in advance I could tell you what I was going to study. We are not talking about that. One of the freedoms I have found was to surrender control of my devotional life to God and give Him the right to change my plans. Now I am more relaxed about it and I enjoy devotional time a lot more.

Common devotional practices

In the devotional life, every great man and woman of God through history has had four common practices and many of them have had a fifth one. These common practices are:

1. Regular study of the Bible.
2. An active growing prayer life with God.
3. Memorization of scripture.
4. Meditation on God's word.
5. A written spiritual journal.

Expect

Come to your devotional life with an open and expectant attitude. Expect to find God there. He has called and He is waiting for you. He wants that appointment with you so expect Him to be with you and to speak to you. Expect Him to touch your heart with His Word.

God said, "If you look for me in earnest, you will find me when you seek me. I will be found by you" (Jeremiah 29:13, 14). It is His promise. You'll find Him there.

Listen

When seeking God, stop to listen to Him and what He has to say. Don't make it just a one-way conversation. For many of us, prayers are like emergency telephone numbers or a catalogue wish list. Instead, we should stop and listen to God, and expect Him to guide.

Be honest and open

As Ellen White wrote, "Prayer is opening the heart to God as to a friend" (*Steps to Christ*, page 93). So what do you tell a close friend? We tell them anything and everything.

This means it is OK to be angry with God and to tell Him so. He knows you are anyway, so why not be honest with Him?

YOU CAN'T FIGHT WITH GOD AT A DISTANCE.

You can't fight with God at a distance. We fight best with Him inside the circle of His arms. That's what Jacob found out that night as he wrestled with God (see Genesis 32:22-32). There are some questions God cannot answer at that time. But it is enough to know that He never lets go of us.

The real test of our spirituality is not the good times but when we experience those dark times and hang on to God through them. In order to do that, I have had to be able to express myself to God and tell Him exactly what I was feeling.

Study

Bible study should not just be about getting to know facts. Rather we should read the Bible to discover the God of the Bible.

For example, which book in the Bible tells us the most about God? Most people can't guess, so think about the book of Revelation. No book in scripture has more names for God and more descriptions of God than the Book of Revelation. It is almost the summary of the entire Old Testament.

Remember how it starts out: "This is a revelation from Jesus Christ, which God gave him concerning the events that will happen soon. An angel was sent to God's servant John so that John could share the revelation with God's other servants. John faithfully reported the word of God and the testimony of Jesus Christ—everything he saw"(Revelation 1:1, 2). It is a revelation about Jesus Christ. We usually study this book to **BIBLE STUDY SHOULD BE A SEARCH FOR THE GOD OF SCRIPTURE.** understand the end of time. That isn't bad, but why not go back and study it meditatively, devotionally, looking for the God of Revelation. And that is how we should study the Bible. Bible study should be a search for the God of Scripture.

Memorize

We should saturate our minds with God's Word—and memorization is one way to do this. Have a plan and a regular process.

It has been proven with intelligence tests that memorization of scripture and studying scripture will actually improve your intelligence scores. It works. Our memorization ability might be rusty but we can put it to work and it will improve.

Meditate

Meditation is simply going into the Word of God and spending time with the content of the passage, reflecting on the depth of its meaning. Or you can take a narrative story and imagine yourself as one of the characters or a spectator in that story, and use your imagination to picture the scenes of that story. When we do this, the words of the Bible come alive to us in new ways.

Pray

Pray before the throne of God. He invites us: "So let us come boldly to the throne of our gracious God. There we will receive his mercy, and we will find grace to help us when we need it" (Hebrews 4:16). Imagine going arm and arm with Jesus, clothed in His righteousness before the throne room of heaven and saying, "God, I am answering your call. I am coming boldly before you in Jesus' name." Imagine talking to Him in Heaven.

We are not creating something new. We are simply accepting who God is—and He creates something new in us, renews our minds and our lives.

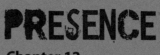

PRESENCE
Chapter 12

In recent years, quite a number of Christian writers have been exploring spiritual formation as a core component of the life of faith. It is another way of talking about and understanding discipleship. Spiritual formation is about opening every part of life to God and letting Him work in our lives. We let Him do what He wants to do in us and grow more like Him, so we draw closer to Him.

Spiritually formed

Spiritual formation has four dimensions:

1. Vision

By vision, we mean a picture of God and who we are in Him. It was this vision that drove many of the men of faith in the Bible. For example, Hebrews 11 describes Moses: "Moses kept right on going because he kept his eyes on the one who is invisible" (Hebrews 11:27).
The bigger and clearer our vision of God is, the easier it is for us to walk with God. And the better our vision of who we are in God, the easier it is to walk with God.

2. Gospel
The gospel is the good news that Christ has solved the sin problem. By faith, the gift is ours—and we have salvation now.

3. Lordship

As we have seen, lordship is about God's right to ownership in our lives. He has the right to be in control of and to guides our lives.

4. Presence

Remember, Jesus said, "I am with you always, even to the end of the age" (Matthew 28:20). He is with us every moment of our lives, not because we feel it but because He said it.

These four dimensions overlap at the cross.
In the cross, we have the clearest vision of God.
In the cross, we understand the gospel and understand His lordship best of all.
In the cross, we best experience the presence of Jesus Christ because

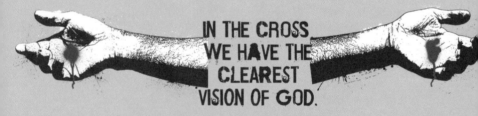

IN THE CROSS WE HAVE THE CLEAREST VISION OF GOD.

in the cross God becomes human and fully shares with us.
Where our vision of God equals our experience of the gospel, our understanding and acceptance of His lordship and our acceptance of His presence in our lives, we grow in oneness with God.

Spiritual trouble-shooting

Most spiritual problems come from either a failure to integrate the gospel into our life or a failure to accept the lordship of Jesus Christ.

But this usually is the result of a problem with vision and presence:

• A loss of vision distorts the gospel.
• A loss of presence distorts the lordship.

So the solution to these problems is to live with vision and presence. It will transform the way we live.

With a clear vision of God and with His presence beside us, we cannot stay the same. The presence and awareness of God's presence in our lives raises sin to what it is—that which interferes with our walk with God.

WITH A CLEAR VISION OF GOD AND WITH HIS PRESENCE BESIDE US, WE CANNOT STAY THE SAME.

A father's story

When my daughter was 19, she was living at home and commuting to an academy about 20 miles away. She would leave about 10:30 in the morning and come home about 9:30 at night.

One evening, I discovered she had been recording a particular TV series and watching it the next morning, when she was home alone before she left for the day. It was a TV series that could be easily described as just one sin after another, so I was concerned—and upset.

HE REACHED INTO MY HEART AND SAID, PRACTICE WHAT YOU PREACH

When she arrived home that night, I said, "Honey, come sit beside me."

"What is the matter?" she asked.

I told her I had noticed that she had been recording the TV program.

"So what?" she said. "I am 19 years old. I am an adult. I can do what I want to. I am old enough to make my own decisions. I can watch what I want to watch.

Her response bothered me. "That's my television," I said. "This is my house. I am paying for the electricity. As long as you are in my house, watching my television, with my electricity, you are not going to watch that."

A fight erupted, both of us with raised voices.

But as our argument continued, I realized what I was saying: "If you don't do it my way, you can get out." Her only option was to defend herself.

I am so glad the Holy Spirit works even in those times. He reached into my heart and said, *Practice what you preach.* I said quietly, "Time out."

"What's the matter?" she said, not sure what I was playing at.

"You are right," I said. "I am wrong. Please forgive me."

Her mouth dropped open.

"You're absolutely right," I continued. "You are 19 years old. You are old enough to make your own decisions. You are an adult. You ought to be making your own decisions about what you watch. Please forgive me."

Now I knew my daughter has a good vision of God. As parents, we have worked over the years to try to improve the picture of God our children have. I also knew she understood the gospel because on several occasions, we have presented the gospel to our children to lead them to accept Jesus as their personal Savior. We did it regularly as a family.

I also knew the lordship issue was clear. She knew she shouldn't have been watching that. Of course, that's why she had been so defensive. My pushing just triggered a sensitive point. So knowing how people grow and function spiritually, I knew what was missing was the presence of God to give her the victory.

"Honey," I said, "if Jesus was visibly beside you, how would it be when you watch that program?"

"Oh Dad," she said quietly, "I don't think I would enjoy that."

"Why not?" I asked gently.

"Because He wouldn't enjoy it and if He wasn't enjoying it, I wouldn't either," she said.

I KNEW WHAT WAS MISSING WAS THE PRESENCE OF GOD TO GIVE HER THE VICTORY.

"But, honey," I prompted, "hasn't Jesus said, 'I am with you always, even to the end of the world'?"

She began to cry. "I know, I know," she sobbed, "but it is so hard. I try so hard and I can't. I try and try—and I can't."

So I said, "Try to lift your right arm"—and she lifted her arm.

"You see, there is no such thing as *try*. You either do or don't. And when it comes to sin, it doesn't matter how hard you try, you never will gain the victory. Because only God can. If you will let Him, He will give you the victory. Honey, do you think you can do that?"

"Yes, I can do that," she said.

"Would you like to do that?" I asked.

She said yes and together, we knelt on the floor in our family room, put our arms around each other and prayed. She asked God to take over and to walk into that area of her life and give her victory.

Whatever area of life we are talking about, the living presence of God becomes real and changes our lives. It is up to us whether we are going to practice His presence or not. It is that simple.

Do we choose to live in Him, with His presence beside us? Or do we try to do it on our own?

A student's story

Back in college, I was feeling miserable one Friday. I had been working an average of 50 to 55 hours a week. And I had a heavy class

load. I had failed a Greek quiz that
morning and I knew it. There were
challenges at work and struggles
with a girlfriend.

That night, I took her to the Friday
night meeting and we walked back
to the dormitories. But I don't know if
I said eight words to her either way. We
got back to the dorm and I realized the last
place I wanted to be was the dorm on Friday
night.

I went to the dean and asked for a leave pass.
Surprisingly, he gave me leave that night.

He asked where I was going and I told him I didn't know, that I
was just going for a drive.

"GOD, I NEED YOU TO RIDE BESIDE ME."

He asked who I was going with. I
told him I was going alone—but
with God. And I told him I didn't
know how long I would be gone.

If I had been that dean, I don't think I would have signed that leave
pass. But he did.

I went out to the car and it was one of those few evenings in college
when it had snowed that afternoon and there was still snow on the
ground. A full moon was out and it was shining brilliantly across the
snow.

I went to the car and opened the passenger's door. I said, "God, I need
you to ride beside me. I need you tonight like I have never needed
you before."

I shut the door and walked around to the other side of the car, got in
and started driving.

I drove back roads for almost three hours before I again recognized
where I was. To get there, I had to have crossed a major highway at

least once—but I didn't remember it.

All I remember is wandering through the back roads, talking to God. I can't tell you that He talked to me audibly but I can't tell you He didn't. He was obviously there with me because He promised. And I talked with Him, opening my heart to Him. A Bible verse would come to mind and I would repeat it and think about it. A chorus would come to mind and I would sing it.

Three hours later, when I realized how far away I was, I decided I had better head back. When I pulled into the parking lot of the dorm, I parked the car. I told Him thank you for riding with me then went around, opened the door and let Him out.

I had still failed my Greek quiz. I still had an extra hard workload. I was still struggling with my girlfriend. But I knew God was with me—and I could deal with the other issues with His presence.

ALL I REMEMBER IS WANDERING THROUGH THE BACK ROADS, TALKING TO GOD.

His transforming presence

All over the world, I have had the privilege of teaching this skill as something we can all practice, even in the ordinary moments of our everyday lives.

I have friends who use traffic lights as a prompt. They drive a lot and every time they come to a red light, it is a trigger to stop and think about the presence of God.

I have another friend who is a housewife. She uses a certain doorway and every time she goes through that door in the house, she thinks about the presence of God. It is something simple to trigger the mind to her heavenly reality.

When we learn to open our lives to God's presence, we begin living in intimate partnership with Him. Everything changes, which is what stewardship is all about.

God-centered living means:

• Allowing God to be God.
• Maintaining confidence in God.
• Accepting God's view of reality.
• Depending on God and His ability to provide.
• Accepting God's boundaries for life.
• Accepting the crucifixion itself and focusing life through Him.

So what will your life be like as you implement this intimate partnership with God in a deeper way?

What would your church be like with more people who are living with awareness of the real presence of God?

How could God touch your life and make a difference?

EVERYTHING
CHANGES,
WHICH IS WHAT
STEWARDSHIP IS
ALL ABOUT.

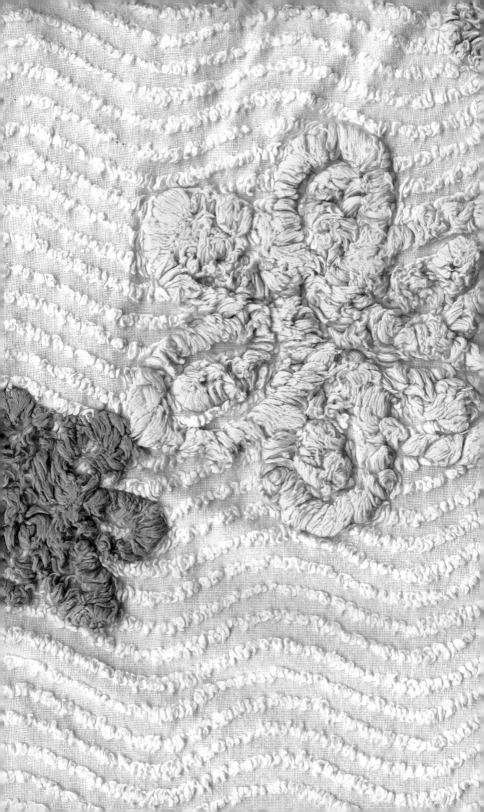

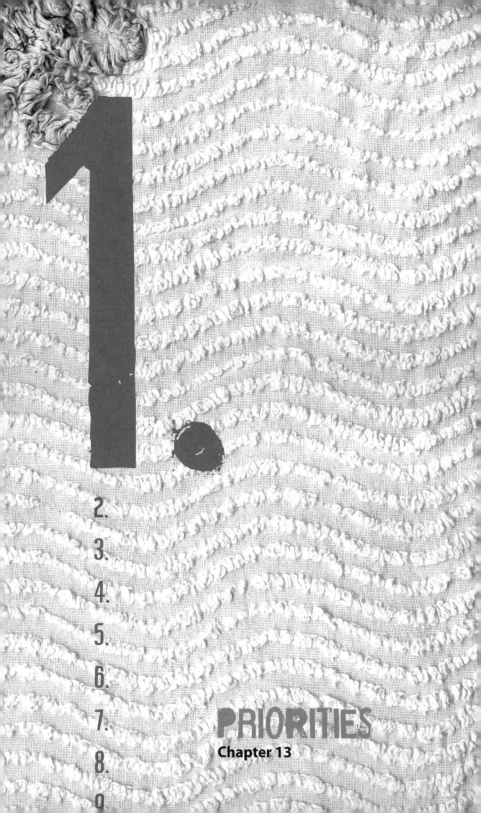

1.

2.

3.

4.

5.

6.

7.

8.

0

PRIORITIES

Chapter 13

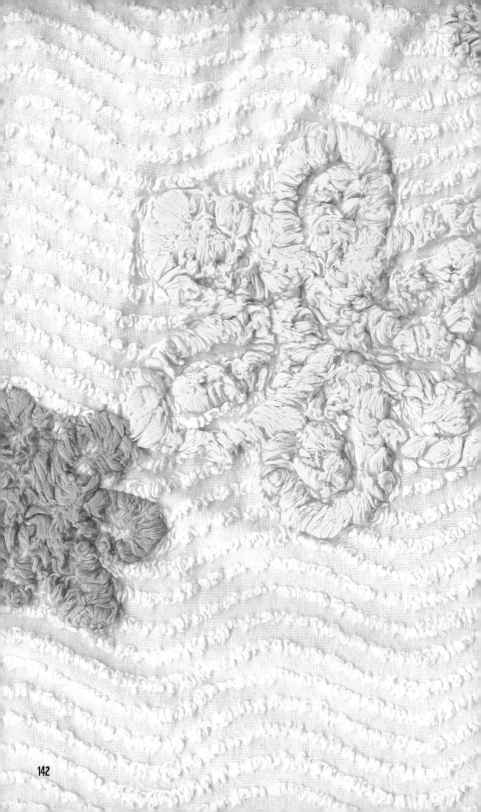

There are 12 principles we have explored in this book that set priorities for making choices in all aspects of our life and faith—our "normal Christianity." When we choose to live as disciples of Jesus, these priorities will change how we think, how we relate to other people, how we spend our time, how we arrange our finances, how we care for our health and will have an impact on every choice we make.

Lordship

Letting Christ be Lord has been a dominant theme of this exploration. There is only one Lord and no one else can be in charge. Christ is Lord of all or He is not Lord at all. It is that simple.

But love is the foundation of this Lordship relationship, without which it is just slavery.

It is like when I put together a swing set for my children. I thought I should be able to put something like that together. So I got it all together but I had a handful of left over pieces. The swing set looked good but it wobbled all over the place.

When all else failed, I went back and read the directions and discovered the handful of pieces I had were the supporting units that went inside some of the other components to make them rigid, to lock them together.

When all else fails, let's read the directions. Let's go back to the basics of the walk with God and let Him be in control.

Ownership

Only God is owner and He is owner of all. We are only managers, trustees or stewards and we have the privilege of managing in partnership with him. God wants us, not just our gifts.

God—first and last

Jesus said, "Seek God first and He will provide" (see Matthew 6:33).
We must make Him first. If anyone or anything else comes first in life, we are practicing a form of idolatry. Putting Him first places everything else in His context. Making Him first and last assures that everything remains in Him.

Making God first and last means we put Him first in life now and after we die. We make provisions for what happens to our possessions after death, including God even in this planning. God makes a difference from the beginning of life until everything He has placed in our hands is back under His guidance in some way or another.

Present

God is with us. Christ has promised to be with us at all times. The Holy Spirit brings the presence of Christ into our lives and we accept His presence by faith.

There are wonderful moments in our lives when we feel His presence. But can I believe He is with me even when I don't feel His presence? This is the present principle.

Pilgrim

We don't belong to this world. We are only resident aliens here. This world is it not our home. We are only pilgrims on earth. We belong to a better land, a better kingdom—and it is already ours. We are already on the throne of Christ, living in the light of eternity. We face the day as visitors in this world and we live by the principles of heaven.

Debtor

Paul said that salvation makes us debtors to God (see Romans 8:12). And because of what Christ has done for us, we are debtors to those around us and we are called to a lifestyle of sacrificing ourselves to God.

Cheerful attitude

Stewardship is about attitude more than mere actions. It begins with loving, not giving. Stewardship means Christ provides the example for how we are going to live. And His was an attitude of open surrender, open giving, openly placing Himself in His Father's hands.

Open hand

If you were to close your hand right now, how many marbles do you think you could hold with your hand closed like that? Perhaps two or three? Now open it and cup it. How many can you hold that way?

An open hand gives God ownership and control, as well as giving Him room to put more in there or to take it out as He wills.

A closed hand also implies ownership, so how we hold what He gives us demonstrates who is in control of "our" lives and "our" stuff.

Big shovel

We can't out-give God. God emptied heaven in giving His Son. And the more we give, the more He can place in our care.

Multiplication

God multiplies the effect of what we surrender to Him. Remember the story of the widow's offering in Mark 12:41-44. She only placed two mites in the offering at the temple—but it was all she had. But God had multiplied that effect over the years as He has used her story to inspire countless others to give with a similar attitude and generosity.

As we surrender to Him and practice stewardship, we grow. Our trusting Him grows. Our spiritual gifts grow. Our ability to give time, talent, energy and ourselves to Him grows. And our relationships grow—with others as well as with God.

Vision

It can take practice but it is living as though we are seeing the invisible. We see God at work in everything around us. We trust that He is there.

We also can begin to see from the reality of God's perspective and begin living from the throne of God. We accept His view of us. Eternal realities break through the present realities. We are not just dependent on or confined to what we are dealing with here.

Partnership

We are created to be dependent on God. Paul wrote, "For I can do everything with the help of Christ who gives me the strength I need" (Philippians 4:13).

Can you imagine anything left out of that? That includes everything—all things.

We are part of the bigger fold, the body of Christ, and we work with other believers. But Christ does not ask us to work for Him—we are not employees, we are partners.

This is the normal way to live with God and by accepting all He offers us, we begin to get normal. And that will transform our lives.

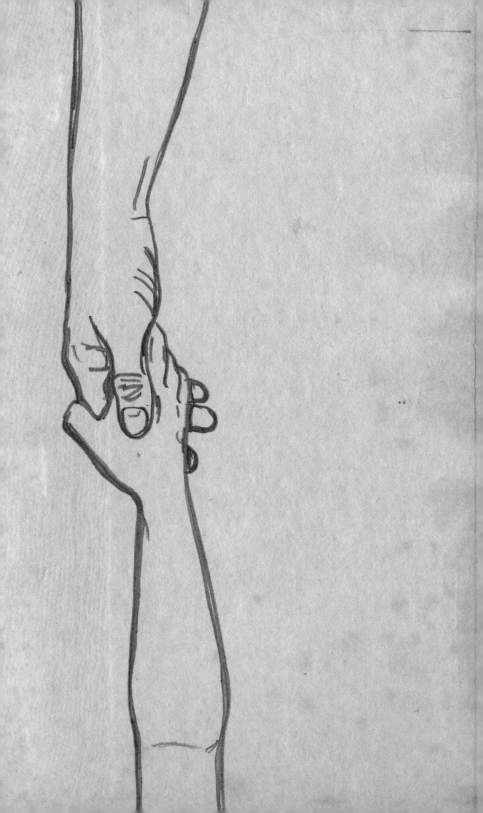